THE TRUTH IS

1. Leveling up your craft to write a story that lives long after you've left the planet is what some might call a ridiculous goal.

2. You will not tell that story after reading just one how-to-write book.

3. You will not tell that story as the result of taking one seminar.

4. You know creating a timeless work of art will require the dedication of a world-class athlete. You will be training your mind with as much ferocity and single-minded purpose as an Olympic gold medal hopeful. That kind of cognitive regimen excites you, but you just haven't found a convincing storytelling dojo to do that work.

5. The path to leveling up your creative craft is a dark and treacherous one. You've been at it a long time, and it often feels like you're wearing three-dimensional horse blinders. More times than you'd like to admit, you're not sure if you're moving north or south or east or west. And the worst part? You can't see anyone else, anywhere, going through what you're going through. You're all alone.

WELCOME TO THE STORY GRID UNIVERSE

HERE'S HOW WE CONTEND WITH THOSE TRUTHS

1. We believe we find meaning in the pursuit of creations that last longer than we do. This is *not* ridiculous. Seizing opportunities and overcoming obstacles as we stretch ourselves to reach for seemingly unreachable creations is transformational. We believe this pursuit is the most valuable and honorable way to spend our time here. Even if—especially if—we never reach our lofty creative goals.

2. Writing just one story isn't going to take us to the top. We're moving from point A to Point A^{5000}. We've got lots of mountains to climb, lots of rivers and oceans to cross, and many deep dark forests to traverse along the way. We need topographic guides, and if they're not available, we'll have to figure out how to write them ourselves.

3. We're drawn to seminars to consume the imparted wisdom of an icon in the arena, but we leave with something far more valuable than the curriculum. We get to meet the universe's other pilgrims and compare notes on the terrain.

4. The Story Grid Universe has a virtual dojo, a university in which to work out and get stronger—a place to stumble, correct mistakes, and

stumble again, until the moves become automatic and mesmerizing to outside observers.

5. The Story Grid Universe has a performance space, a publishing house dedicated to leveling up the craft with clear boundaries of progress and the ancillary reference resources to pack for each project mission. There are an infinite number of paths to where you want to be, with a story that works. Seeing how others have made it down their own yellow-brick roads to release their creations into the timeless creative cosmos will help keep you on the straight and narrow path.

All are welcome—the more, the merrier. But please abide by the golden rule:

Put the work above all else, and trust the process.

HAMILTON BY LIN-MANUEL MIRANDA

A STORY GRID MASTERWORK ANALYSIS GUIDE

ABIGAIL K. PERRY

Edited by
SHEILA LISCHWE

STORY GRID

STORY GRID

Story Grid Publishing LLC
223 Egremont Plain Road
PMB 191
Egremont, MA 01230

First Story Grid Publishing Paperback Edition
March 2021

For Information About Special Discount for Bulk Purchases,

Please visit www.storygridpublishing.com

Paperback ISBN: 978-1-64501-060-9
Ebook ISBN: 978-1-64501-053-1

For

All Past, Present, and Future Story Nerds

HOW TO READ HAMILTON BY LIN-MANUEL MIRANDA: A STORY GRID MASTERWORK ANALYSIS GUIDE

1. Watch the performance and enjoy it without worrying about any of the Story Grid stuff.

2. Then, watch each scene thinking about the Story Grid principles. Each scene is identified by the song(s) included.

a) At the conclusion of each scene in this Masterwork Analysis Guide is a section entitled *Analyzing the Scene*. By answering four Socratic questions, I'll walk you through how to determine the critical information for the Story Grid Spreadsheet—*Story Event* and *Value Shift*.

b) Another section I've included at the end of each scene is "How the Scene Abides by the Five Commandments of Story-telling."

For each and every scene in *Hamilton*, I indicate the Inciting Incident, Turning Point Progressive Complication, Crisis, Climax, and Resolution.

For those unfamiliar with Story Grid's Five Commandments of

Storytelling, you can read about them in the book *Story Grid 101* (free download on the Story Grid site), in *The Story Grid: What Good Editors Know*, or in articles about them on the site. Just access the "start here" or "resources" section of https://www.storygrid.com/ to read at your leisure.

c) In addition to the Story Grid Spreadsheet for *Hamilton*, you can view the Story Grid Foolscap and the actual Story Grid Infographic at https://www.storygrid.com/masterwork/Hamilton/.

INTRODUCTION

Hamilton, Lin-Manuel Miranda's Broadway phenomenon, has been a major success since its debut in 2015.

While the musical quickly rose to great heights and still reigns as a Broadway darling, people laughed when Miranda announced at a White House Poetry Jam that the cast would perform "a song from the hip hop album they were working on ... 'about the life of somebody who embodies hip hop—Treasury Secretary Alexander Hamilton.'"[1]

Disney paid seventy-five million dollars to acquire worldwide distribution rights and released it on Disney+ more than a year earlier than planned, in July 2020.[2].

It's also garnered critical acclaim. As this Masterwork Guide goes to press, *Hamilton* has won eleven Tony Awards, a Grammy for best musical theater album, a Pulitzer Prize for drama, and was nominated for the NAACP Image Awards and two Golden Globes.

How do we explain this level of success? Interest in the historical figure himself couldn't account for the show's popularity. Before the musical, it wasn't uncommon for people outside of Wall Street, politics, and teaching to remember Hamilton, one of the founding fathers of our nation, only for his last act. Hamilton died in a duel against Aaron Burr.

I'm not the first person to ask this question, and there are some obvious answers. Beloved by most Broadway fans, *Hamilton* is often adored for the magic of revolutionizing Broadway with hip hop (and teaching history at the same time!), its emphasis on cast diversity, and incorporating interculturalism.[3] The protagonist and antagonist are bound in political and personal struggles while the story celebrates America's history told by contemporary Americans.[4] Because of this, *Hamilton* has made its own contribution to history.[5]

The story works for our time, though it concerns historical events. The infectious and clever music, talented and diverse cast, and energetic action scenes followed by quiet contemplative ones make this story a crowd pleaser.

But is there more to it than that? If you took these advantages away, would it be just another story we enjoy and forget? I don't think so.

The foundation of *Hamilton* is a solid story that focuses on striving individuals dreaming of and working toward a better life and legacy. It is a perfect example of what we call a *Status* Story in the Story Grid Universe.

While *Hamilton* is still a relatively new story (can you believe the musical has been around for only six years as this guide goes to press?), it has all the hallmarks of one that will endure and resonate with people across culture and time.

We call stories like these *masterworks* because we can study them to better understand what makes certain stories resonate long after their creators have died. These stories become legacies because their plots, characters, and messages are not bound by contemporary popularity—and therefore transcend time.

---

1. "Remarks by the President at 'Hamilton at the White House,'" March 14, 2016, https://obamawhitehouse.archives.gov/the-press-office/2016/03/14/remarks-president-hamilton-white-house.
2. Erich Schwartzel, "Disney+ Takes Its Shot at 'Hamilton' Movie with Early Online Debut," *The Wall Street Journal*, May 13, 2020, https://www.wsj.com/articles/hamilton-movie-to-debut-on-disney-july-3-11589294497.
3. Brian Rowe, "Why is Hamilton so Successful?" November 22,2018, https://medium.com/@brianrowe_70270/why-is-hamilton-so-successful-71e1752257f6.
4. Rowe, "Why Is Hamilton so Successful?"

5. Jeremy McCarter and Lin-Manuel Miranda, *Hamilton: The Revolution* (New York: Grand Central Publishing, 2016).

HOW LEGACIES ARE MADE

Hamilton is a masterwork, but how do I know? What qualities show this? To answer, we need to look at the story from different angles and altitudes. Let's start with the basics.

Hamilton is the story of the rise of a penniless orphan who becomes the first Treasury Secretary of the United States. Later, he is involved in a sex scandal that leads to self-sabotage and death in a duel at the hand of Aaron Burr, one of his oldest friends.

That's pretty compelling! But there's a lot more to Hamilton's life and career than this summary suggests.

It is also the story of how Hamilton struggles to survive abandonment by his father and later his mother's death. He writes about the devastation to his hometown in the Caribbean by a hurricane, and people raise money to send him to college in America. He rises to become Washington's personal secretary during the Revolutionary War, establishes the nation's financial system (that's still with us today), and writes to influence the 1800 election.

Along the way, he meets and marries his soulmate, Eliza, and they build a happy life and family. Hamilton later betrays Eliza, and they lose a son, but she forgives him, and they reconnect after their loss.

It's also the story of an underclass revolting against a tyrant who drains their resources and wealth and imposes unreasonable restrictions and burdens on the citizens, and how the colonists battle Britain, a global superpower, in a war to forge a new nation and way of life.

How does Miranda weave these threads together without creating a muddled mess? I'm so glad you asked! The reasons this story is greater than the sum of its exciting and intriguing parts do not have to remain a mystery.

One simple answer is that the story abides by what we story nerds in the Story Grid Universe call the conventions and obligatory moments of the global genre, and the scenes are executed flawlessly to create a pattern of change our human brains recognize. I'll spend the rest of this Masterwork Guide explaining exactly why this story works so well by using Story Grid tools to examine the story as a whole (what we call the global story) in this introduction, followed by a thorough analysis of the individual scenes. As I lead you through the scenes, I'll point back to the global story so you can see how Miranda is weaving the story lines together.

Hamilton's development and production are well documented. In *Hamilton: The Revolution*, writer and critic Jeremy McCarter and Miranda help us go behind the scenes to see how the masterpiece was crafted. (Be sure to get yourself a copy—every Ham-Fan needs one!) Also hundreds of written and recorded interviews reveal *Hamilton* is the product of hundreds of artists working to express their individual gifts together to create a transcendent work of art.

This story analysis isn't meant to take anything away from the brilliant contributions of others, but when we analyze a masterwork, we focus on the story itself because that is a record of the decisions the writer made. Understanding *why* a master writer makes decisions, in the context of the story's structure, helps us, as writers, make our stories a little better. Novelists don't have the benefit of stunning visuals, talented actors, and memorable music that come with a Broadway musical, but we still have a lot to learn from *Hamilton*.

In this Masterwork Guide, I analyze the story itself using a handful of my favorite Story Grid tools to provide multiple perspectives on the work. I hope this will help you see *Hamilton* in a new way, through a writer's lens, and show you how to analyze other stories so you can see all stories in a new way.

WHAT'S THE GLOBAL GENRE?

How do we sort out all these story threads? How can we understand the story better so Miranda's work can serve as a mentor to us as we write our own stories?

First, we understand that no matter how many subplots a story contains, it has only one global content genre.[1] The global genre is what the story is *really about*. This keeps us from going astray. If the global story is strong enough, it can support other subplots that create a richer experience and a variety of conflict. *Hamilton* has four clear subplots, which I described in the paragraphs above. They include Performance, Love, Society, and War. Can you match the paragraphs to these content genres? Even if you're new to Story Grid, you can probably figure it out.

But what is the story really about?

If we step back and look at the story's main conflict, what do we have? This is the story of the rise and tragic fall of Alexander Hamilton. Miranda had many options among the different content genres he could use to tell *Hamilton*, but as written, this is what we call a *Status Tragic* story.

Most audience members couldn't tell you that, but they can recognize it by distinct qualities—a certain type of character, who faces a certain challenge and ends up a certain way. With a Status Tragic story, a striver makes a mistake that dooms him or her to failure.

More specifically, we could say *Hamilton* is the story of the rise of a penniless orphan who becomes the first Treasury Secretary of the United States but later is involved in a sex scandal and dies in a duel at the hand of one of his oldest friends.

This is the basic pattern of change we see in a Status Tragic story.

We can spot this trajectory in other stories, including the Greek myth of Icarus, which Eliza mentions in "Burn," Theodore Dreiser's *An American Tragedy*, Edith Wharton's *The House of Mirth*, and in characters like Stannis and Renly Baratheon in *A Song of Ice and Fire* by George R.R. Martin.

Each of the twelve Story Grid content genres have qualities we describe with the Four Core Framework. The elements of this framework (the core need, core value, core emotion, and core event) help us take fundamental story structure and function and make it specific to each genre. They help us understand why we're attracted to certain types of stories.

- The Core Need (survival or esteem, for example, based on Maslow's Hierarchy of Needs)
- The Core Values (a range from life to death or impotence to power, for example, which shows us how the protagonist is doing in meeting their core need)
- The Core Emotion (excitement or admiration, for example, which is the emotional change in the audience when the protagonist gets what they need—or not)
- The Core Event (a scene demonstrating proof of love or a showdown between the protagonist and antagonist, for example, when we see the protagonist's ultimate decision to obtain what they want or attain what they need)

We read Status stories because we want to know if the protagonist (which we call the luminary agent), will rise in social standing and achieve society's definition of success at the expense of their self-respect or discover and embrace their personal definition of success.

In these stories, an unexpected event (the global inciting incident) offers an opportunity or challenge and awakens the protagonist's desire to improve their circumstances in life. The protagonist wants success and third-party validation as well as the rewards that come with them, and they are unaware they need self-respect.

The unexpected event changes their situation along a gradient of value that goes from negative to positive, *failure to success*. Between success and failure, the protagonist's situation may land on the contrary value of *compromise*. Beyond failure in a negative direction is *selling out*. We call this the negation of the negation because it's a negative value appearing positive.

In Status stories, we relate to the protagonist because we understand the need for *respect* but also the desire for success. We wonder what this protagonist is willing to do to achieve society's definition of success and if they will get the respect they need (because we face the problem of how to thrive too). We can judge how well the protagonist is doing in meeting the need throughout the story by identifying where they sit on the gradient of value—from *failure* to *success*.

We admire the protagonist who sticks to their personal moral code when it conflicts with getting what they want and improving their status or circumstances. If the protagonist abandons their code to secure loftier heights, we feel pity. *Admiration* or *pity* are the core emotions we experience in Status stories depending on what the protagonist chooses.

Every scene brings the protagonist closer to or further from success, but the most important scene is what we call the *Core Event*, or the *Big Choice* moment that comes near the end of the story. In this moment, the protagonist's need for respect is in the most jeopardy. We get a solid idea of where they will land on the value gradient between failure and success, and we feel admiration or pity because they gain respect or not.

---

1. For more information about the twelve content genres, *see* Shawn Coyne, *The Four Core Framework: Needs, Life Values, Emotions, and Events in Storytelling* (Egremont, MA: Story Grid Publishing, 2020).

STATUS STORY'S SUBGENRES

The Status genre concerns the protagonist's attempt to rise in social standing and what they are willing to sacrifice to do so.

As you can imagine, this can work out well or not so well. It's a matter of realizing that getting what we want will never satisfy our needs (simple but not easy!). The choices we make in life matter, and while those choices are often limited by factors beyond our control (for example, the weather or the decisions of kings or colleagues), we can always choose to follow our personal moral code to attain our need for respect.

Status stories are divided into four subgenres depending on the luminary agent's strength of character and choices.

The *Admiration* subgenre features a strong, sympathetic, and principled protagonist who refuses compromise and succeeds despite the misfortune they face. Examples include *A Little Princess* by Frances Hodgson Burnett, Peter Maas's *Serpico,* or the 2000 film *Gladiator.* You can also see this character arc at work as a secondary genre in *Catching Fire* by Suzanne Collins (Katniss Everdeen) and *Leviathan Wakes* by James S.A. Corey (James Holden). In *Hamilton,* Eliza and Washington are Admiration characters that provide contrast to Hamilton's own character movement.

The *Sentimental* subgenre features a weak protagonist who nevertheless succeeds because they remain steadfast in following their code and the advice of one or more good mentors. Colm Tóibín's *Brooklyn* is a great example, and films include *Rocky* (1976), *Real Women Have Curves* (2002), and *Puzzle* (2018).

The Pathetic subgenre features a weak protagonist who attempts to achieve success, but fails, as in Thomas Hardy's *Tess of the d'Urbervilles*. We see this character arc operating as a secondary genre in *Ethan Frome* by Edith Wharton (Ethan Frome). Burr follows the Status Pathetic arc. He consciously avoids taking a principled stand. This passive approach to getting what he wants and his willingness to wait make him a perfect antagonist to oppose Hamilton.

The Tragic subgenre features an ambitious protagonist or striver whose mistakes doom them to failure. This is Hamilton's story. Other good examples include Theodore Dreiser's *An American Tragedy* and the 1951 film adaptation, *A Place in the Sun* and Wharton's *The House of Mirth*. Stand-out characters who rise and then fall because of a tragic mistake include Cersei Lannister in the television series adaptation of Martin's series of novels, *Game of Thrones*. And don't forget the Greek myth and cautionary tale of Icarus.

STATUS STORY'S CONTROLLING IDEA

The controlling idea or theme of any story is the primary lesson the audience receives by the time they reach the end. This brief statement also captures the change that happens in the story and why.

For a Status story, we say generally, *"Staying true to one's own values, whether or not this leads to social betterment, defines success. But if one sells out, exchanging their values for meaningless rank, praise, or acquisitions, the result is failure."*

With the Tragic subgenre, we can say more specifically, when a protagonist is ambitious and understands the consequences of their actions but sacrifices their personal code while trying to improve their circumstances, they suffer a tragic fall.

But our story doesn't end with Hamilton's death—thanks to his devoted and loyal wife, Eliza.

Eliza not only ensures her husband's legacy as a founding father but tells the stories of the men who fought for him. In the fifty years after Hamilton's death, she dedicates her life to major achievements that today exist as national treasures, including the Washington Monument and the first American orphanage in New York City. She acts out of unconditional love for her late husband because the care of her family is central to her moral code. Despite the pain he caused while alive, Eliza longs for her husband—loving him beyond his death and until her end.

To account for this final story movement, we can say:

Failure results when a striver sells out for unworthy goals, but if a heroic figure picks up the torch and preserves his story's lessons, humanity is enriched.

Since we're never told this explicitly, how does Miranda help us get this message? Every scene transmits the truth of this controlling idea, but the heavy lifting happens through genre conventions, which set our expectations and set up the obligatory moments that pay them off.

STATUS STORY'S CONVENTIONS

To set up the change we describe in the controlling idea and put the core need at stake, we must create the right environment, populate it with the right kinds of characters, and add the right circumstances. That may sound formulaic, but it's story form that we can feel and recognize and expect. These constraints cause external conflict to arise, and when combined, they ultimately force the protagonist to choose between pursuing the status they want and the respect they need.

Let's look at the global conventions in *Hamilton*. First, we need the right setting.

Big Social Problem as Subtext: What kind of environment can cause external conflict that forces Hamilton to choose between outer success and his personal moral code? The hurricane in the Caribbean is an unexpected event that gives rise to an unexpected opportunity to go to America. The Revolutionary War also provides opportunity, as Hamilton predicts it will. Stressful events like natural disasters and war allow people with skills and determination a chance to perform. But that doesn't mean the rewards for service are distributed fairly. New opportunities create intense competition for what seem to be limited resources. And class and racial prejudice make it harder for people to improve their circumstances. As an immigrant, Hamilton struggles to elevate his status in a society that values people's social standing. That's why accepting Washington's offer to serve as his right-hand man was so important for Hamilton's rise in status. (But notice that Washington's support also caused jealousy among Hamilton's colleagues.)

Within the story's setting, archetypal characters perform specific functions in the protagonist's life.

Strong Mentor Figure: A mentor is a character who creates chaos for the protagonist by challenging them to grow and fulfill their potential. Why is this important in a Status story? A protagonist who seeks to rise within their society faces challenges that require better skills and a more sophisticated worldview. They need someone who has more experience to offer guidance. More than one character can fulfill this role within the story. George Washington is Hamilton's professional mentor who often tries to teach Hamilton that no one has the power to control their narrative after death. Eliza serves as a personal mentor reminding Hamilton that the love of a partner and family can be enough. Notice that these two characters follow an Admiration arc. That's not a coincidence!

Shapeshifters as Hypocrites: A shapeshifter is a character who appears to be one way and turns out to be another. Burr fulfills this role in the story and is a great example of this archetype. One obvious example of this in action is when he switches political parties to run against Philip Schuyler after he is excluded from the negotiations in "The Room Where It Happens" (scene 25). But he tells us up front in "Aaron Burr, Sir" that he's a shapeshifter. "Talk less. ... Smile more. ... Don't let them know what you're against or what you're for." By not committing to anything, he can't be pinned down or contradicted.

These characters also create chaos for a Status Story protagonist. Hamilton is trying to learn the ropes of the extraordinary world he's been granted access to, and shapeshifters create a destabilizing effect that forces the protagonist to question what they think they know about the world. Hamilton wants to like Burr because of what they have in common, but Burr's unwillingness to take a side or pursue the woman he loves creates cognitive dissonance in Hamilton.

The Herald or Threshold Guardian: This character is a fellow striver who has sold out. They appear near the boundary between the ordinary world where the protagonist knows how things work and the unfamiliar extraordinary world. This character informs the audience the rules are about to change by telling the protagonist (or other character) the way things are. Burr performs this service in "Aaron Burr, Sir" (scene 2), when he warns Hamilton that, "Fools who shoot their mouths off end up dead." Burr continues to fulfill the role throughout the plot, often discouraging Hamilton from revealing too much. Of course, Hamilton often improves his circumstances by speaking up, which we can see in examples like "My Shot" (scene 3), "Farmer Refuted" (scene 6), and "Non-Stop" (scene 20). A threshold guardian like Burr could try to discourage or help the protagonist, but not necessarily. They act to get what they want, and that may align with what the protagonist wants or not.

Once we have the right setting and characters, we need additional circumstances or catalysts to increase the tension and conflict.

A Clear Point of No Return: This moment follows what we call the *All Is Lost Moment* when the protagonist must choose between what they want (success at the cost of their moral code) and what they need (respect that comes from acting consistently with their moral code). In a story like *Hamilton*, this is a tragic mistake that dooms the protagonist because there is no way to reverse it. This happens when Hamilton writes and publishes the *Reynolds Pamphlet* (scene 32). Once he does this, he sabotages his family and his career (not to mention Maria Reynolds as well) to prove the point that he "was honest with the money."

Win-but-Lose or Lose-but-Win Ending: Hamilton risks death in the duel against Burr, and then dies because he throws away his shot. At this point, he has contributed to the founding of a new nation, but his enemies try to bury his good work after his death. Luckily, Eliza fights to preserve Hamilton's legacy and is successful, even if she never knows this.

Conventions set up the conflict in the story, but the obligatory moments take the ingredients of conflict and cause change in the core value of the story. Let's look at them next.

STATUS STORY'S OBLIGATORY MOMENTS

Obligatory moments cause change in the story's core value through unexpected events, revelations, decisions, and actions. Every scene must "turn" to cause incremental change in the story that affects the core value for the protagonist. But we expect to see certain special moments in every Status Story that emphasize the change. Notice that Hamilton's antagonist Burr often appears during these pivotal events.

An Inciting Opportunity or Challenge: After writing an impressive account of the hurricane that destroyed his Caribbean hometown, Hamilton is given the money to travel to America to get an education. (Burr is one of the first people he meets when he arrives.)

The Protagonist leaves home to seek fortune: Hamilton travels to America to study and later accepts Washington's invitation to work as his right-hand man in the Revolutionary War. (Burr volunteers his services to Washington and is dismissed when Hamilton arrives.)

Forced to adapt to a new environment, the Protagonist relies on old habits and humiliates himself or herself: Hamilton is frustrated because he is stuck behind a desk during the Revolutionary War. He acts out by accepting the role as John Laurens' second in a duel with Charles Lee. (Burr acts as Lee's second in the duel.)

The Protagonist learns what the Antagonist's Object of Desire is and sets out to achieve it for him or herself: Although Hamilton has several antagonists in the story, the main antagonist in the story is Burr. What's interesting is that Hamilton never really understands Burr because he will say he wants political success but does nothing decisive to achieve it. However, the *audience* learns what Burr's wants and desires are in "The Room Where It Happens" when he admits that he wants to be present where big decisions are happening. In other words, he wants to secure his legacy by achieving political/professional success and status. Hamilton wants this also, and he sets out to do this from the beginning of the story.

The Protagonist's initial strategy to outmaneuver the Antagonist fails: Jefferson, Madison and Burr confront Hamilton because they think he's embezzled Treasury funds. To prove that he's not guilty, he shows them evidence of the real scandal. Hamilton secures their promise to keep the secret to themselves, but Burr says enigmatically, "Alexander, rumors only grow. And we both know what we know." Hamilton has given Burr, his global antagonist, a powerful weapon here. This is important in a Status Story because we need to see how the protagonist reacts to misfortune.

During an All Is Lost Moment the Protagonist realizes they must change their definition of success or risk betraying their morality: Hamilton publishes the *Reynolds Pamphlet*, which backfires immediately. Hamilton thinks revealing his secrets will clear his name, but instead, the public admission ruins his legacy and risks his marriage as well as the reputations of Eliza and Maria. He also ensures he will never again possess the political success he had during Washington's administration.

The Core Event: The Big Choice Moment when the Protagonist realizes they must change their definition of success or reject the world they strived to join. Hamilton throws away his shot in a duel with Burr. In his final moments alive, Hamilton questions what makes a legacy and decides it is more honorable to delope (fire in the air) than to kill Burr. He accepts the risk of death—and then is killed.

The Protagonist saves or loses him or herself based on the Core Event. Hamilton loses his life, but because Eliza recognizes his desire to contribute to the new nation, she tells his story and continues his work in the world.

The obligatory moments create a pattern of change that we recognize as a Status story. But each scene must also contribute to the global story and bring the protagonist closer to or further from the core value. How can we confirm this is happening in a masterwork or in our own stories? Story Grid tools help us analyze any scene to be sure it works.

STATUS STORY UNDER THE MICROSCOPE

Scenes are the building blocks of stories and represent mini-stories of their own. They involve characters doing things (moving and speaking) in pursuit of a goal and in conflict with other characters or the nature of the environment. This conflict causes characters to act, and those actions cause change.

When we identify the actions, conflict, and change in a scene, we see the small decisions a writer like Miranda makes to build the story. In our own stories, we determine whether the scene is affecting the core value, success in a Status Story, or whether the scene should be eliminated. We combine action, conflict, and change in a short, specialized summary we call the *Story Event*.

To be more precise, we say, a Story Event is an active change of a universal human value for one or more characters as a result of conflict. (One character's desires clash with another's, or an environmental shift changes the value positively or negatively.)

A Working Scene contains at least one Story Event. To determine a scene's Story Event, we answer four Socratic questions. You'll find my answers to these questions for every scene in *Hamilton* following this introduction.

STORY EVENT

1. What are the characters literally doing—that is, what are their micro on-the-surface actions?

We say this is what the characters are literally *doing*, but it also includes what they are *saying*. This is pretty straightforward and might include having a conversation, eating a meal, fighting a duel, or speaking to a crowd.

For instance, in "Aaron Burr, Sir," (scene 2), Hamilton meets Burr outside a bar and seeks his advice. He also meets Laurens, Lafayette, and Mulligan.

This is different from what the characters want or are trying to achieve in the scene (that's the subject of the next question). The on-the-surface action is how characters go about getting what they want.

Later, in "My Shot," (scene 3) Hamilton wants to impress his three new comrades, but what he's *literally* doing is drinking in a bar and discussing the Revolution.

Character action evokes excitement in us because it's focused on *how* they pursue what they want (which we can relate to) and is all about what is happening now in the story's *present*. Keep in mind the actions a character takes say a lot about who they are and what they believe. This is important for character and plot development.

2. What is the essential tactic of the characters—that is, what above-the-surface macro behaviors are they employing that are linked to a universal human value?

As writers we need to think about what characters do but also why they do it. This is what we're getting at with the *essential tactic*. What do the characters in the scene want? Scenes require conflict, and that means characters must want different things. At least one active character in the scene must experience at least one force of antagonism that prevents the primary character we're following from easily getting what they want. This desire at the scene level should align with what the character wants at the story level, which we call their *conscious object of desire*.

In "Aaron Burr, Sir" (scene 2), Hamilton wants to graduate early and hopes Burr can advise him. Burr wants Hamilton to follow a cautious path to keep him out of trouble. That doesn't make sense to Hamilton, though. Inside the tavern, Laurens, Lafayette, and Mulligan share who they are and what they stand for. They want Burr to do the same, but he declines.

This antagonist can be another character(s), the weather, or mechanical failure. It can even be internal conflict, but something external must force that to the surface. The key here is that whoever or whatever the antagonist is, they must complicate the main character's journey by forcing them to make decisions. These decisions cause change, which is the subject of the third question.

On the global (macro) scale, Hamilton wants to elevate his status and achieve success that will secure his legacy. Despite his relentless drive and exceptional intelligence, he can't control how people remember him after his death or even what people say about him now. His denial or misunderstanding of this reality supports and complicates his progress on a scene-by-scene basis.

The essential tactic is about what the character wants for the *future* and is based on how they see the world and themselves. We often pick this up between the lines or in subtext. Characters don't always reveal their essential tactics because it could interfere with getting what they want when other characters oppose them. But it also serves a story purpose. Readers experience intrigue because they don't know (but want to know) why characters do what they do. This makes them keep reading to find out!

3. **What beyond-the-surface universal human values have changed for one or more characters in the scene? Which one of those value changes is most important and should be included in the Story Grid Spreadsheet?**

The decisions characters make transform them and their situation. And when we talk about *value* and *polarity* shifts, this is what we mean. Think of universal human values as descriptive words used to explain how the main character(s) in the scene have changed, including their external circumstances or their internal condition from the beginning to the end of the scene. In "Aaron Burr, Sir," (scene 2) there is a shift from *Eager to Learn* to *Rejecting Advice*. This reflects Hamilton's internal state of hope to disappointment as well as his external circumstances because he has chosen to stay true to himself.

Again, the character's choices advance the plot, causing the change we can describe—from positive to negative or vice versa. We look at how that positive or negative movement affects the global value, which in a Status Story is success. In our example, Hamilton's success is enhanced by rejecting Burr's advice because it causes Laurens, Lafayette, and Mulligan to notice him. Notice that Hamilton doesn't know this in the moment. We view the scene from the perspective of knowing the entire story.

Small scene-level changes must affect the global value, or the scene will distract from the story. Both the value shift description and the polarity shift are added to the Story Grid Spreadsheet so we can track change in the story.

Positive influences and actions result in desirable outcomes, like Hamilton's decision to work for Washington in "Right Hand Man" (scene 7) or marrying Eliza at the end of "Helpless" (scene 8). But his actions also result in self-sabotaging decisions like publishing his affair in the *Reynolds Pamphlet* (scene 32).

The variety of negative and positive shifts make the story engaging and push Hamilton forward in the story. The ups and downs allow the audience to vicariously experience this emotional movement too. We see this scene to scene, but in the Story Grid Infographic you can see Hamilton's overall trajectory from the beginning to the end.

One of the best ways to identify this shift is to look at the scene's Turning Point Progressive Complication. (More on that soon!) The turning point is the moment in a scene when the universal human value begins to shift, and it forces the character into the dilemma we call the Crisis.

A scene may include several value shifts. Multiple characters may experience changes in their situation, and those changes could be external or internal. When you analyze a scene, the way you describe these shifts is up to you! Often, a shift is in the eye of the beholder. But if you focus on how the global value is enhanced or threatened, you should be in good shape.

4. **The Scene Event Synthesis: What Story Event sums up the**

scene's on-the-surface actions, essential above-the-surface world-view behavioral tactics, and beyond-the-surface value change? We will enter that event in the Story Grid Spreadsheet.

The Story Event is a short summary that brings the other three components together in a meaningful way. The Story Event does for the scene what a logline or controlling idea does for the entire story. It shows us what's important so we can immediately begin to see why the scene is in the story. You could also say it answers the question: How do the answers to the first three questions show us the key point of the scene? How does a character get closer to or further away from their goal because of how they tackle their antagonist/obstacles?

Crafting a Story Event can be intimidating. Don't be concerned if you feel confused or overwhelmed! Take your best guess and know there is no one single right answer. You can always make adjustments as you deepen your understanding of the story. Masterworks aren't analyzed in a day, and the skills needed to read critically like a writer will take time to develop as well. Luckily, you have this Masterwork Guide to help sharpen your analytical skills!

I've summed up "Aaron Burr, Sir," with this Story Event: *Hamilton meets Burr for the first time and asks how to get ahead, but Hamilton openly rejects that advice.*

Now that you have your Story Event, wouldn't it be useful to understand how the writer incorporates the action, conflict, and change in the scene? The Five Commandments of Storytelling will help you do just that.

HOW THE SCENE ABIDES BY THE FIVE COMMANDMENTS OF STORYTELLING

Within each story unit there is a pattern of change we call the Five Commandments of Storytelling. Here's a brief description of each one from *Story Grid 101*.

- The Inciting Incident, which kicks off the action in the story, scene, or other story unit;
- The Turning Point Progressive Complication, an unexpected event that turns the human value at stake in the scene, and gives rise to . . .
- The Crisis, which is a dilemma about how to confront the unexpected event;
- The Climax, which is the decision and action a character takes in response to the Crisis; and
- The Resolution, which is the outcome of the action of the Climax.

Let's go a little deeper and see how this works in our example "Aaron Burr, Sir" (scene 2).

Inciting Incident

The global inciting incident is an unexpected event that upsets the protagonist's life in the ordinary world. Within a scene this event changes a character's circumstances but on a smaller scale. (As a general rule you can think of scenes as mini stories with smaller causes and effects that add up to the macro action and change of the entire story.) In "Aaron Burr, Sir," Hamilton runs into Burr and introduces himself.

The inciting incident could be simple like this one or complex as well as positive or negative from the main character's perspective. In the analysis, we identify inciting incidents as causal or coincidental. Does a character cause the inciting incident or is it just something that happens? Hamilton is hoping to meet Burr, so the inciting incident of scene 2 is causal.

You may encounter a scene where the inciting incident happens off stage, or we join a scene where the action is already in progress or "in media res." Writers can avoid what's obvious because it's clear from the context. For example, in "The Room Where It Happens" (scene 25), we don't see Jefferson and Madison invite Hamilton to meet, but we assume from the context that they did.

The inciting incident should cause the character to want something, even if that is a desire for things to go back to the way they were before. The character translates this desire into their essential action in the scene. For example, in the scene "Aaron Burr, Sir," Hamilton wants to graduate early, so when he meets Burr, he pursues this goal by asking for advice. This becomes important as we talk about Progressive Complications.

Turning Point Progressive Complication

Progressive Complications happen when something in the environment responds to the protagonist or point of view character's pursuit of a goal (essential action). The complications could be obstacles that stand in the way of achieving the goal or tools that help them. For example, college officials will not permit Hamilton to graduate early (obstacle), but he and Burr have something in common (they are both orphans), and that could make Burr want to help Hamilton (tool).

One particular complication, an unexpected event, allows the character to *make sense of* the inciting incident in a new way. It could be character action or a revelation in the mind of the character. This is the Turning Point Progressive Complication, which creates a situation that keeps the protagonist from reaching their goal in the way they'd planned, sparking the dilemma we call the Crisis.

The Turning Point Progressive Complication in scene 2 comes when Burr offers Hamilton some advice that surprises him. Burr tells him to "Talk less. Smile more." In essence, Burr suggests that if Hamilton wants to improve his situation, he should not insist on graduating early or join the army. This raises Hamilton's Crisis in the scene.

Crisis

The Crisis boils down to an either/or question—a dilemma—that might be large or small depending on the story unit but forces the character to choose. The Crisis could be between two negative options (a best bad choice) or between options that may be good for one party and bad for another (irreconcilable goods choice).

Within a scene there may be multiple crises for the different characters, but when we analyze a scene, we follow one character in particular, usually the protagonist.

In scene 2, Burr has an irreconcilable goods choice when Hamilton asks for advice. Burr can choose to help Hamilton or not. Helping out is good for Hamilton, but it takes Burr away from his plans for the evening. He chooses to offer the advice (Burr's scene-level Climax), which becomes Hamilton's Turning Point.

When Hamilton hears the advice, he must choose whether to accept or reject it. He has a best bad choice. He doesn't want to offend Burr, who has offered him a drink and advice, but Hamilton can't accept the advice and be true to himself.

Climax

The Climax of a scene is the decision and action the character takes when faced with their best bad choice or irreconcilable goods choice.

In "Aaron Burr, Sir," Hamilton chooses to reject Burr's advice when he says, "If you stand for nothing, Burr, what'll you fall for?"

Resolution

A resolution is what happens in the environment as a result of the climactic action. We always need to know the result of the choice, even if it comes a little later.

In the case of "Aaron Burr, Sir," Hamilton's climactic action comes in the final line of the song. The Resolution follows at the beginning of the next song, "My Shot," which is part of the next scene. Laurens, Lafayette, and Mulligan hear Hamilton's response to Burr. They are impressed and want to know more about him. They say, "Ooh, who is this kid? What's he gonna do?" When they ask these questions, we begin to wonder too.

THINK LIKE A WRITER

Analyzing stories doesn't only help you become a better writer. It helps you become a better reader and thinker.

One of the most disappointing realities I faced during my years teaching was how disinterested students are becoming in reading. This is partly because they feel spread too thin to actually read and partly because they are shackled by the need to read for a test instead of for growth, learning, and entertainment.

When I was in high school, I loved reading but often felt drained by reading assignments because I didn't really know how to read for long-term comprehension. I finally realized I needed a reason to *care about* what I was reading in order for the content to stick with me.

And while my reading abilities strengthened in college, it wasn't until I found Story Grid—and then became a certified editor—that I *actually* became a reader who read with a purpose.

I learned how to read like a *writer*.

This renewed focus and mindset—to read like a writer—has had a monumental impact on my ability to question and understand *why* a plot moves and works. This gives me a lot more confidence to discuss *how* the scenes and story do this.

People have built-in story receptors because stories are an important part of the way we learn and survive. But reading, writing, and storytelling are learned skills—ones that go hand in hand. You can't become great at one without practicing the others.

(**Special shout out to teachers!** Reading stories with a focus, like the Story Grid scene analysis, is perfect for the Common Core curriculum, especially when it comes to pulling out key ideas and details and integrating knowledge. I hope to share more about this soon!)

A word of caution: Doing a close analysis of a masterwork, including a scene-by-scene breakdown of a favorite story, is a time-consuming and difficult process. There's a large learning curve when it comes to Story Grid tools and terminology. You need to keep asking questions. (The Socratic method is key!) This is why the Story Grid Methodology is so useful. We use practical tools and storytelling principles to support our analysis instead of regurgitating ideas that have been said before.

When we share our thoughts on what advances the plot, how a character develops, or the value and polarity shift in a scene, we must accept that our answers may be different from those of other people who read the same story. It's okay to disagree! As long as we agree on common terminology and an understanding of story principles, we can respect *why* someone believes a scene moves forward in a certain way (or doesn't), even if we see it differently.

When you study a story this closely, you may find your favorite story has some flaws you didn't realize were there. That doesn't mean something is wrong with you. Few works of art are perfect.

You may find a beloved story loses some of its magic because you see how the writer makes you feel the way you do when you read or watch it. I think this offers us a deeper appreciation, a mature love and respect for the commitment and craft that goes into art that does more than show us a good time.

If you accept the challenge to analyze a story you *love*, I promise you'll become a better storyteller because of your hard work. And what's even more special, you'll likely develop an intimate, personal relationship with the narrative because you'll have spent so much focused time with it.

We can all learn something personal and valuable from a deep study of great stories. I probably won't ever meet Lin-Manuel Miranda, but I've spent so much time with *Hamilton* and taken my best guess at why it works that it's like getting the opportunity to learn from him directly.

If you decide to take on your own masterwork analysis, I commend you! The work of studying and analyzing great stories and writing your own stories is so valuable. If you dedicate yourself to the craft, your passion and time will pay off.

SCENE ANALYSIS

"ALEXANDER HAMILTON"

SCENE 1

SUMMARY

The opening scene of *Hamilton* introduces the protagonist, Alexander Hamilton, with an overview of his tragic youth narrated by important figures in his life, including his global antagonist, Aaron Burr. He poses a central question. How can someone from a small town in the Caribbean who is so disadvantaged grow up to be a person of great consequence?

Hamilton is an orphan born out of wedlock whose father leaves when he is ten. His mother dies from an illness Hamilton survives, and he is forced to move into his cousin's home. When his cousin commits suicide, he is left with nothing, and Hamilton realizes the only way to escape his poverty is to get an education. He reads a lot and works for his late mother's landlord until a hurricane destroys his town.

Devastated, Hamilton writes about the hurricane's destruction. His work catches the attention of a group of men who offer to pay for his trip to New York and college expenses. Hamilton seizes this opportunity and sails away to begin his new life.

As Hamilton travels, other characters share highlights of what's to come. We hear from the men who will fight with him, the men who die for him, the women who will love him, and Burr, who will take his life.

3

The opening scene ends with Hamilton's ship arriving in New York Harbor.

ANALYZING THE SCENE

STORY EVENT

A Story Event is an active change of a universal human value for one or more characters as a result of conflict (one character's desires clash with another's, or an environmental shift changes the value positively or negatively).

A Working Scene contains at least one Story Event. To determine a scene's Story Event, answer these four Socratic questions:

1. What are the characters literally doing—that is, what are their micro on-the-surface actions?

Alexander Hamilton's friends, family, and enemies recount his origin story as he works toward a better life by studying, working, and writing.

2. What is the essential tactic of the characters—that is, what above-the-surface macro behaviors are they employing that are linked to a universal human value?

Hamilton wants to be a part of something bigger than himself, but his situation presents many hurdles, like being born out of wedlock and later becoming an orphan. He strives to overcome his circumstances by educating himself and working for his late mother's landlord, and he writes an essay after a hurricane destroys his home.

3. What beyond-the-surface universal human values have changed

for one or more characters in the scene? Which one of those value changes is most important and should be included in the Story Grid Spreadsheet?

Identifying the most important value change in a scene is sometimes difficult. When in doubt, the Story Grid rule of thumb is to highlight the value that best aligns with the progress of the global human value at stake in the story. *Hamilton* is a Status Story, which has a global value at stake of *Failure/Success*. In the Story Event analysis, we'll make note of different changes in the lives of the characters, but in the Story Grid spreadsheet, we'll track the ways Hamilton's ability to succeed is threatened or enhanced scene by scene.

Driven by his will to overcome his disadvantages, Hamilton learns to "fend for himself" after his father abandons him, his mother dies, and his cousin commits suicide. When Hamilton writes about the hurricane that destroys his town, some people offer to pay his expenses to attend college in America.

In this scene Hamilton begins in the Caribbean and ends in New York City as a result of his hard work. The choice is clear. We'll track insignificant to recognized in the value shift column of the spreadsheet. Even though the words are different, they suggest change from *failure* to *success*.

Insignificant to Recognized

4. The Scene Event Synthesis: What Story Event sums up the scene's on-the-surface actions, essential above-the-surface worldview behavioral tactics, and beyond-the-surface value change? We will enter that event in the Story Grid Spreadsheet.

The audience learns Hamilton's origin story—from his father's abandonment to Hamilton's voyage to the new land and his obsession with legacy.

HOW THE SCENE ABIDES BY THE FIVE COMMANDMENTS OF STORYTELLING

Inciting Incident: Causal. When Hamilton is ten years old, his father abandons him and his mother.

Turning Point Progressive Complication: Active. Hamilton's cousin commits suicide, leaving him with nothing—alone and penniless.

Crisis: Best bad choice. Hamilton can fend for himself or accept a life of squalor.

Climax: Hamilton decides to educate himself. He borrows and reads books while working for his late mother's landlord. After a hurricane destroys his town, he publishes what he writes about it.

Resolution: A group of men are impressed by Hamilton's writing about the hurricane. They offer to pay for his travel and college expenses.

NOTES

- Miranda dramatizes Hamilton's intelligence and willingness to work hard, and these explain some of his ability to overcome the disadvantages of his circumstances. However, other people apply their intelligence too. The question that Burr poses throughout is how did he do it? This is a perfect focus for a *Status Story* where we're concerned with what people are willing to do to achieve their subjective definition of success. The key to Hamilton's success is his obsession with legacy. He's concerned with third-party validation and how people will think and talk about him after his death. This is his *conscious object of desire,* or what he wants from the beginning of the story. It drives him relentlessly not just to improve his circumstances but to be part of something bigger than himself and to earn respect of people he's never met. "The world's gonna know your name."
- Status Story protagonists experience misfortune repeatedly, and we see that in this first scene. Hamilton is clearly challenged by his unfortunate circumstances, including

abandonment, loss, destruction of his home, remote location, and debt. None of these affect his likelihood of success as much as his cousin's suicide, which is the Turning Point Progressive Complication of this scene. When Hamilton is alone, he accepts that only he can pull himself out of his life of squalor. The action of his cousin's death sparks the revelation that he needs to "fend for yourself." This is an example of an *active* turning point causing a *revelation* because the unexpected event forces the character to make sense of what happened in the inciting incident. Hamilton's father left him, but that doesn't immediately lead him to the revelation that he must think and work for himself. While the most assistive action in the scene comes when men help Hamilton to further his education, the opportunity arises only because Hamilton chooses to take responsibility for himself. It's the arena's response to his climactic action, or the Resolution.

- In a Status Story, a protagonist can earn success in one of two ways, *prestige* (influence or reputation) or *dominance* (when status is demanded). To provide balance and contrast in these stories, writers might change the protagonist's approach or add an antagonist who strives for success in the opposite way. (Remember, the antagonist is the protagonist of their own story!)

- Hamilton elevates his status in this opening number through prestige. Someone gains prestige when they do something to earn the respect and attention of others. They might establish this through achievements and/or relationships. Hamilton works, studies, and writes until a group of men recognize his exceptional intelligence and potential.

- Hamilton's obsession helps him because he needs a lot of agency (the ability to identify and solve problems) to overcome the challenges he faces. He's like a rocket trying to escape Earth's gravity. But his obsession also hurts him because learns too late that there is a time to be relentless and a time to wait. This complication makes this a Status-Tragic Story. The tactics that propel him from a small town in the Caribbean to George Washington's side will not serve him in other situations, and he fails to recognize this.

- Status Stories pair well with Performance, Society, and War subplots because the conventional settings of those stories involve clear hierarchical structure and characters looking to improve their circumstances by gaining agency. It's not a coincidence that many scenes in *Hamilton* include the conventions and obligatory moments of all three, and I'll point them out in the notes. Don't forget the Love Story! Adding elements of other genres through subplots is a great way to add dimension to a story. It's vital to choose a single global genre and deliver all its requirements, but once you've accomplished that, you can add interest with the ingredients from other genres.

- What can we make of the decision to reveal the ending (Burr kills Hamilton) in the first scene? Miranda understood audience members would know the result of Hamilton's duel, even if they don't have many details about his life. Knowing how the story ends changes the question that keeps the audience interested in the story. We know *what* will happen, so we wonder *why* and *how* it will happen. We call this the form of narrative drive, and here, Miranda uses *dramatic irony*, where the audience knows more than the characters. Successful writers choose the questions they want readers or audience members to think about, and then structure the story to direct attention to the events that dramatize the answers to the questions.

- Fun Fact: The men who put up the money for Hamilton to attend college in New York did so hoping he would return to the Caribbean where he could use his knowledge to improve his homeland. He never made it. But this inspired Miranda to bring *Hamilton* to the Caribbean after the original Broadway run concluded to raise money and provide support for the islands.

"AARON BURR, SIR"

SCENE 2

SUMMARY

Hamilton studies at King's College and is desperate to graduate early so he can join the army and fight for the revolution.

He encounters Burr and asks how he successfully graduated early. Burr shares that it was his "parents' dying wish." Hamilton reveals that he is an orphan also and longs to go to war to prove his worth.

Burr offers Hamilton some advice that stuns him. "Talk less. Smile more." At first, Hamilton thinks Burr is joking but is disappointed as he learns the man is serious.

Burr offers John Laurens, Marquis de Lafayette, and Hercules Mulligan as examples of men who risk their opportunity for success because they will likely die in the war. Hamilton dreams of martyrdom, so death fails to scare him. Instead, he becomes fascinated by the other three men and listens as they introduce themselves, their passions, and their intentions. The four men together see the war as a chance for glory, freedom, and success.

When Laurens challenges Burr to share his story and goals, Burr declines. Hamilton is baffled. "If you stand for nothing, Burr, what'll you fall for?" Laurens, Lafayette, and Mulligan recognize Hamilton as a kindred spirit and wonder what he will do.

ANALYZING THE SCENE

STORY EVENT

A Story Event is an active change of a universal human value for one or more characters as a result of conflict (one character's desires clash with another's, or an environmental shift changes the value positively or negatively).

A Working Scene contains at least one Story Event. To determine a scene's Story Event, answer these four Socratic questions:

1. What are the characters literally doing—that is, what are their micro on-the-surface actions?

Hamilton meets Burr outside a bar and seeks his advice. While there, he also meets Laurens, Lafayette, and Mulligan.

2. What is the essential tactic of the characters—that is, what above-the-surface macro behaviors are they employing that are linked to a universal human value?

Hamilton wants to graduate from college early and hopes Burr has the answer to how he can accomplish this. Burr advises caution, encouraging Hamilton to "Talk less. Smile more," which is contrary to everything Hamilton believes about rising to the top. Laurens, Lafayette, and Mulligan's desires are aligned with Hamilton's.

3. What beyond-the-surface universal human values have changed for one or more characters in the scene? Which one of those value changes is most important and should be included in the Story Grid Spreadsheet?

Desperate to graduate early and elevate his status, Hamilton is hopeful as he seeks advice from Aaron Burr, a man he admires. But Hamilton doubts Burr's advice and ultimately feels disappointed. Burr declines the invitation from Laurens, Lafayette, and Mulligan to "drop some knowledge." Hamilton then challenges Burr's strategy on how to become successful. By doing so, Hamilton catches the attention of the other three men, which sets him up to gain success through prestige and on his own terms.

Again, in the Story Grid spreadsheet, we focus on the ways Hamilton's ability to succeed is threatened or enhanced scene by scene.

Here, Hamilton starts out eager to learn from Burr, someone he thinks is like him but further along the path. He ends up rejecting Burr's advice because it's contrary to his beliefs.

Eager to Learn to Rejecting Advice

4. The Scene Event Synthesis: What Story Event sums up the scene's on-the-surface actions, essential above-the-surface worldview behavioral tactics, and beyond-the-surface value change? We will enter that event in the Story Grid Spreadsheet.

Hamilton meets Burr for the first time and asks how to get ahead, but Hamilton openly rejects that advice.

HOW THE SCENE ABIDES BY THE FIVE COMMANDMENTS OF STORYTELLING

Inciting Incident: Causal. Hamilton introduces himself to Burr and asks how he graduated from college early.

Turning Point Progressive Complication: Active. Burr advises Hamilton to keep his opinions to himself if he wants to get ahead. He also declines the opportunity to say who he is, what he believes in, and what he wants as Laurens, Lafayette, and Mulligan have done.

Crisis: Best bad choice. Following Burr's advice means Hamilton denies his own instincts and potentially fails in life, but disagreeing with Burr could risk his friendship with someone who could help him.

Climax: In the last line of the song, Hamilton openly rejects Burr's advice by saying, "If you stand for nothing, what will you fall for?"

Resolution: The resolution comes at the beginning of the next song, "My Shot," when Laurens, Lafayette, and Mulligan ask Hamilton who he is and what his plans are. This gives Hamilton a chance to prove his intelligence to them, and he won't decline the opportunity as Burr did.

NOTES

- Although Hamilton publicly rejects Burr and his advice, the universal human value moves toward *success*. This is because Hamilton gains attention by doing the unexpected. Burr and Hamilton are established as foils. Both want success and need esteem, but how they move forward is different and determines their decisions and actions as they rise and fall. Setting up differences between a protagonist and antagonist —while also showing how they are similar—is a brilliant way to build tension in a relationship. It's a perfect recipe for conflict!
- Remember, the protagonist in a Status Story can achieve success through prestige or dominance, and the antagonist often pursues success in the opposite way from the protagonist. This scene, where Hamilton and Burr first meet, establishes their different approaches. At this point in the story, Hamilton cannot achieve success through dominance because he has no real power to exercise. This is why he seeks Burr's advice on how to graduate early. The only way to improve his circumstances is to impress his superiors, like Burr did. But Burr has other significant advantages that make it possible for him to wait. Even though he's an orphan, he is a gentleman who comes from a wealthy and

powerful family. He uses privilege (dominance) to get ahead.

- What's equally interesting about Burr is that he does not demand power actively like the common antagonist asserting his dominance to gain success. Instead, Burr advises Hamilton that the only way to achieve success is by hiding what he really believes and holding his tongue when he disagrees with his superiors. "Talk less. Smile more." This interaction reveals an important dynamic between them. Hamilton knows the revolution is coming and will not miss his opportunity. Burr prefers to wait for the right time and place before acting. Burr's warning that "fools who run their mouths wind up dead" will ring true at certain moments in the story, but as observers, we know Burr becomes "the damn fool who shot" Hamilton. Death might not get Burr first, but his bitterness toward Hamilton because he gains success through bold action will be Burr's downfall as much as Hamilton's death flows from his inability to pause and reflect.
- Because we know Burr shoots his friend Hamilton, Burr's story is not about whether he will shoot Hamilton but why does he shoot Hamilton? A fantastic plot choice! We start to understand the mystery of why Burr shot Hamilton here. No way will Hamilton adopt his new friend's strategy (at least, not yet). Hamilton's success tortures Burr. He fails to achieve success by taking the more sophisticated approach.
- Notice that the Resolution for this scene occurs in the next song, which is part of the next scene. Writers sometimes choose to split a scene across multiple chapters, or songs, or include multiple scenes within a chapter or song. In novels, this is often done to adjust the pace of the story. While scenes are the building blocks of stories, chapters are the building blocks of books, and songs are the building blocks of a musical.
- Burr offers Hamilton some advice that stuns him: "Talk less" and "Smile more." This is Burr's moto throughout the story.

It suggests that the best way to get ahead is to keep your opinions to yourself—the exact opposite of what Hamilton expects or wants to hear. At first, Hamilton thinks Burr is joking but becomes increasingly disappointed as he learns Burr is serious.

- Miranda notes that this encounter is reminiscent of the scene in *Harry Potter and the Sorcerer's Stone* when Harry meets Draco Malfoy in Diagon Alley.[1] Writers who want to deliver a powerful scene look to great examples of similar events. They can strip away the details to see what's really happening. Two rivals meet for the first time on the antagonist's turf. Even though there are lots of differences (a young adult fantasy novel versus a historical musical employing factualism), we can glean tips on how to craft a scene that satisfies.

---

1. McCarter and Miranda, *Hamilton: The Revolution*, 24n5.

"MY SHOT" AND "THE STORY OF TONIGHT"
SCENE 3

SUMMARY

After being questioned by Laurens, Lafayette, and Mulligan, Hamilton takes center stage to declare who he is and what he wants.

Hamilton unapologetically proclaims he is, "not throwing away my shot!" Hamilton sees the war as his opportunity to "rise up" and establish his legacy by leading soldiers in battle or dying as a martyr. He encourages others to support the war. Laurens, Lafayette, and Mulligan join Hamilton, impressed by his ability to speak and persuade.

Burr interrupts to warn that they might be killed before they've accomplished anything. Hamilton challenges Burr, and his passion wins the others over. Laurens says they should put his skills to work converting others.

As the new friends drink shots at the bar, they declare they will seize their current opportunities. A crowd of colonists joins them. Laurens tells them to "rise up," and Hamilton explains the revolution, offering the chance to contribute to something meaningful and be a force for good.

At the end of this energetic night, the new friends sing alone in the bar about the glory they may never see but will fight for anyway.

ANALYZING THE SCENE

STORY EVENT

A Story Event is an active change of a universal human value for one or more characters as a result of conflict (one character's desires clash with another's, or an environmental shift changes the value positively or negatively).

A Working Scene contains at least one Story Event. To determine a scene's Story Event, answer these four Socratic questions:

1. What are the characters literally doing—that is, what are their micro on-the-surface actions?

Hamilton drinks in a bar with Laurens, Lafayette, and Mulligan while recruiting colonists to fight in the revolution.

2. What is the essential tactic of the characters—that is, what above-the-surface macro behaviors are they employing that are linked to a universal human value?

Hamilton wants to prove he possesses the fiercest intellect in the room. He does this by sharing both his strengths and vulnerabilities with the crowd and recruiting them to join his quest to fight in the revolution. He wins over his new buddies, particularly Laurens, who suggests they get Hamilton to speak to other potential recruits for the cause.

3. What beyond-the-surface universal human values have changed for one or more characters in the scene? Which one of those value changes is most important and should be included in the Story Grid Spreadsheet?

Hamilton's new friends are skeptical at first as Hamilton confesses his lack of status, wealth, and power, which he considers a liability. But Hamilton's status among his peers quickly rises as he earns their admiration and sways the colonial bystanders. Even Burr seems impressed with Hamilton's ability to influence the crowd, and though Burr argues against the outspoken tactics, he is soon forgotten.

Failure to Success

4. The Scene Event Synthesis: What Story Event sums up the scene's on-the-surface actions, essential above-the-surface worldview behavioral tactics, and beyond-the-surface value change? We will enter that event in the Story Grid Spreadsheet.

Hamilton impresses his companions by preaching about the colonists' need for war and why he is the right person to lead the people into a fight for freedom, all while literally taking shots in a bar. Later, he and his companions sing about their dreams of glory late into the night.

HOW THE SCENE ABIDES BY THE FIVE COMMANDMENTS OF STORYTELLING

Inciting Incident: Causal. Laurens, Lafayette, and Mulligan ask who Hamilton is, pushing him to explain.

Turning Point Progressive Complication: Active. Laurens endorses Hamilton's leadership when he tells everyone to get Hamilton in front of a crowd.

Crisis: Irreconcilable goods choice. Hamilton can speak up and join Laurens, Lafayette, and Mulligan, or he can take Burr's advice and wait for the war to come to them.

Climax: Hamilton takes his place as the leader in this new group. For the first time in his life, Hamilton is "thinkin' past tomorrow," in other words, beyond mere survival. He has found community, brotherhood, and opportunity to fight and live for, and he will sacrifice whatever is required to "rise up."

Resolution: With his new companions, Hamilton sings about their dreams of freedom and how people will tell their story in the future.

NOTES

- It's important to remember that progressive complications don't always need to be negative. The opportunity Hamilton earns in "My Shot" is an important complication in his story. Developing supportive friendships that enhance his success and enrich his life will also complicate his situation because their respect and well-being matters to him. Instead of thinking of complications as negative, think of them as circumstances that make your character's life harder. Hamilton's success increases his psychological, physical, and professional stakes. Hamilton strives for success, but that doesn't mean his life will get easier.
- We know Hamilton's story is told in the future, but he couldn't have known that at the time. He believes he can control what other people say after his death. This is a naïve belief. According to Story Grid's Heroic Journey 2.0, this is a manifestation of what we call his worldview 1.0. This belief will be challenged through much of the story. Hamilton will have the opportunity to upgrade to worldview 2.0 with a focus on the deep meaning of life rather than his legacy. The freedom these friends dream of securing may or may not be within their grasp, but the stories told about their efforts are out of their hands.
- Though Washington is the leader of the colonial army, Hamilton is our central figure in the War Story subplot. This scene shows us the offshoot characters who embody different aspects of Hamilton's personality. Can you see how a scene in a tavern where these friends first connect is a great way to deliver this convention?

- "The Story of Tonight" is part of the Resolution of this scene. There is no value shift in this song, but we see the friends sharing not just their audacious goals but their personal hopes and dreams. This is made possible because Hamilton inspires them all.

"THE SCHUYLER SISTERS"

SCENE 4

SUMMARY

Burr sets the scene and offers his opinion about why wealthy people, particularly the Schuyler sisters, visit poor and working-class neighborhoods. He suggests they want to "gawk" at the poor, students, and working men. We soon learn he has misread the sisters' motivations and misjudged Angelica completely.

Each sister shares her perspective on what's unfolding before them. Peggy is concerned about being in the city without permission and the violence that may erupt if the colonists rebel. Eliza is captivated by the excitement of the moment. Angelica is looking for a like-minded mate with "a mind at work."

When Burr asks Angelica why she is there, she tells him she finds his inquiry offensive. She shares that she's read *Common Sense* and is frustrated with their culture because she believes in equality for everyone, including women. She intends to convince Thomas Jefferson that women's equality is good for society.

ANALYZING THE SCENE

STORY EVENT

A Story Event is an active change of a universal human value for one or more characters as a result of conflict (one character's desires clash with another's, or an environmental shift changes the value positively or negatively).

A Working Scene contains at least one Story Event. To determine a Scene's Story Event, answer these four Socratic questions:

1. What are the characters literally doing—that is, what are their micro on-the-surface actions?

Angelica, Eliza, and Peggy sneak into New York City, despite their father's instructions to be home before dark.

2. What is the essential tactic of the characters—that is, what above-the-surface macro behaviors are they employing that are linked to a universal human value?

Angelica wants to find a man whose intellect rivals her own, someone who will give her a "revelation" and support her quest for women's equality. Her younger sisters go along in support, but Eliza is captivated by everything that's happening, and Peggy is concerned about being there without permission and the violence that will come with war. Burr wants to put Angelica in her place and get her to admit what he thinks she's doing. He represents society as a force of antagonism to women who want to express themselves and be equal to men.

3. What beyond-the-surface universal human values have changed for one or more characters in the scene? Which one of those value changes is most important and should be included in the Story Grid Spreadsheet?

When Burr approaches Angelica, she defends her actions and

beliefs by citing texts like Thomas Paine's *Common Sense*. Meanwhile, Eliza reflects on how lucky they are to be alive right now, and all three sisters join the enthusiasm and determination overtaking the city people.

Hopeful to Dissatisfied

4. The Scene Event Synthesis: What Story Event sums up the scene's on-the-surface actions, essential above-the-surface worldview behavioral tactics, and beyond-the-surface value change? We will enter that event in the Story Grid Spreadsheet.

Angelica ventures downtown in New York City with her sisters to search for a mate who will support her ideals, and she rejects Burr and his advances.

HOW THE SCENE ABIDES BY THE FIVE COMMANDMENTS OF STORYTELLING

Inciting Incident: Causal. Angelica and her two sisters, Eliza and Peggy, sneak downtown.

Turning Point Progressive Complication: Active. Aaron Burr insults Angelica with his inquiry and comments.

Crisis: Irreconcilable goods choice. Angelica can remain subservient, pardoning an acceptable suitor (Burr), or she can defend her intellect and desire for women's equality.

Climax: Angelica defends herself while illustrating her extreme sophistication and intellect. She cites her readings of *Common Sense* and defends her desire for women's equality.

Resolution: Angelica, Eliza, and Peggy reflect on how lucky they are to be alive during this time of revolution and change.

NOTES

- Without the protagonist present, it can be challenging to identify the scene's Five Commandments. A lot is happening on the surface here, but the key to unlock this scene is to look at the subtle change in Angelica's worldview. She is remarkably sophisticated, and this scene gives her an opportunity to speak out for what she wants and believes despite living in a time when women were not often publicly encouraged to do so. Presented with the dilemma to say nothing or speak up, we see she doesn't care much about what men, including Burr, think about her, but she absolutely cares about her beliefs. Angelica symbolizes the energy and determination shared by other minds at work and the people who support the revolution. She shows hope for the promise of tomorrow through her curiosity, drive, and intelligence (much like Hamilton), even if she's unsatisfied from beginning to end. At the same time, she represents the frustration of those who are suppressed by an evolving society.
- This scene reveals Burr's character too. He drops his usual tactic and directly challenges Angelica. He is hopeful of making a connection with Angelica but is disappointed when she turns him down.
- This scene is doing several things though Hamilton never appears onstage and isn't mentioned. (Of course, we can't help thinking of him when Angelica tells us the kind of mate she's looking for. Can we?) We're getting a feel for the setting, or what we call the global arena that gives rise to the conflict in the Society subplot. The people want freedom and feel hopeful about the possibility of revolution. The three sisters represent three different perspectives on what's happening. Angelica sees opportunity, Eliza feels excited, and Peggy feels nervous.
- We're meeting the Schuyler sisters before they meet Hamilton. Eliza is Hamilton's love interest, and Angelica to a certain extent is a rival. Miranda lays the groundwork for the Love Story subplot here.

- Miranda also establishes Angelica as a point of view character in this scene, which will be important later on. Angelica tells Eliza's story just as Eliza tells Hamilton's. What's interesting in light of all the discussion about who tells the story is how difficult it would be to tell one's own story. We don't have perspective. The best we can hope for, really, is that someone who cares for us remembers.

"FARMER REFUTED"

SCENE 5

SUMMARY

As talk of a revolution gains momentum, colonists loyal to the king speak up. One of these men, Samuel Seabury, is an Episcopal rector. He stands on a box in the town square to express his independent opinion or "free thoughts" on the "proceedings of the Continental Congress."

Hamilton, Mulligan, Lafayette, Burr, and others stand to the side watching. Mulligan encourages Hamilton to "tear this dude apart," but Burr advises that they "let him be." Hamilton challenges Seabury's points with rapid-fire retorts.

Hamilton refutes Seabury's arguments and notes how foolish Seabury sounds given the chaos and bloodshed the British have already caused the colonists, which can no longer be ignored.

Hamilton rejects Burr's attempt to intervene. Instead, Hamilton insults Burr, saying he would rather be "divisive than indecisive." The people are swayed by Hamilton's argument. Finally, the heralds enter the scene and demand silence to deliver a message from the king.

ANALYZING THE SCENE

STORY EVENT

A Story Event is an active change of a universal human value for one or more characters as a result of conflict (one character's desires clash with another's, or an environmental shift changes the value positively or negatively).

A Working Scene contains at least one Story Event. To determine a scene's Story Event, answer these four Socratic questions:

1. What are the characters literally doing—that is, what are their micro on-the-surface actions?

Hamilton and Samuel Seabury debate whether the colonists should join the revolution.

2. The Worldview Story Component: What is the essential tactic of the characters—that is, what above-the-surface macro behaviors are they employing that are linked to a universal human value?

Seabury wants to persuade the people that the revolution is wrong. Hamilton wants to humiliate and disarm Seabury. In a public forum, they engage in a verbal joust.

3. The Heroic Journey 2.0 Component: What beyond-the-surface universal human values have changed for one or more characters in the scene? Which one of those value changes is most important and should be included in the Story Grid Spreadsheet?

Hamilton moves from observer in the scene to defender of the revolution as he successfully refutes Seabury's arguments and gains more support from colonists. Seabury meanwhile shifts from confident to humiliated. The value most relevant to the global Status Story is Hamilton's shift from a witness to an influencer.

Witness to Influencer

4. The Scene Event Synthesis: What Story Event sums up the scene's on-the-surface actions, essential above-the-surface worldview behavioral tactics, and beyond-the-surface value change? We will enter that event in the Story Grid Spreadsheet.

Samuel Seabury addresses the public to express his thoughts on the proceedings of the Continental Congress, which Hamilton tears apart in public.

HOW THE SCENE ABIDES BY THE FIVE COMMANDMENTS OF STORYTELLING

Inciting Incident: Causal. Samuel Seabury announces he wants to share his opinion about the actions of the Continental Congress.

Turning Point Progressive Complication: Active. Samuel Seabury jabs at the revolutionists' egos by praying the king will show them mercy.

Crisis: Best bad choice. If Hamilton fights back, he could lose the respect of citizens who, like Seabury, don't believe in the revolution. If Hamilton doesn't fight back, he could lose support from the crowd interested in or unsure about the revolution.

Climax: Hamilton chooses to spar with Seabury—lyrically and literally. Aaron Burr tries to calm the situation, but Hamilton dismisses Burr with the comment that he'd rather be "divisive than indecisive."

Resolution: Hamilton earns the respect of his fellow revolutionists. The king sends the colonists a message.

NOTES

- This scene highlights once again the differences between Hamilton and Burr in temperament and action. The tension between Hamilton and Burr is growing not only because Hamilton rejects Burr's advice but because

Hamilton is successful by being "divisive instead of indecisive."

- Unlike most heroic figures, Hamilton rarely refuses the call to adventure. This is typical for a Status Story protagonist. Instead, they often fail to see the whole truth in the opportunities offered to them. Hamilton acts on impulse and expresses his opinions forcefully, and—as Burr warns—this will get him into trouble (eventually). For much of the beginning, we see him climb toward success with few hiccups. This is true socially and professionally, but not internally as Hamilton feels dissatisfied. In this way, we see Hamilton moving on an "Icarus type" of story arc (Eliza quotes Angelica on this point later in the story). Hamilton is focused on controlling how history sees him and doesn't see the danger in working for third-party validation.

"YOU'LL BE BACK"
SCENE 6

SUMMARY

King George III delivers a threat to the colonists disguised as a love letter. He seems concerned and confused about the colonists' rebellious behavior, like when they hurl tea into Boston Harbor. He questions why the colonists are "so sad" when together they "made an arrangement when" they went away.

Then, he warns them that he's growing angry.

Despite these colonial outbursts, the king is certain his subjects will return to him. He trusts that in time they will remember their shared experience and connection as well as his service to them. But he also warns if they don't back down, he will send a "fully armed battalion to remind [them] of [his] love."

The king trails off into a singsong melody, "da da da da," that contrasts his underlying message about the imminent danger of challenging him. If the colonies rebel, they will go to war with a global superpower. King George III treats the colonists' grievances as if they are the complaints of a naïve child who doesn't really know what they're doing, and with this arrogance he sincerely believes the colonies will give up.

A British soldier then kills the first colonist.

ANALYZING THE SCENE

STORY EVENT

A Story Event is an active change of a universal human value for one or more characters as a result of conflict (one character's desires clash with another's, or an environmental shift changes the value positively or negatively).

A Working Scene contains at least one Story Event. To determine a scene's Story Event, answer these four Socratic questions:

1. What are the characters literally doing—that is, what are their micro on-the-surface actions?

King George III sends the colonists a warning.

2. What is the essential tactic of the characters—that is, what above-the-surface macro behaviors are they employing that are linked to a universal human value?

King George III wants to retrieve what he thinks is rightfully his—the colonies and his "loyal subjects." He sends a love letter of sorts to communicate his anger, but the colonies don't surrender.

3. What beyond-the-surface universal human values have changed for one or more characters in the scene? Which one of those value changes is most important and should be included in the Story Grid Spreadsheet?

King George III shares his apparent sadness and disappointment in his subjects. This disappointment becomes insane anger the more he thinks about the colonists' misbehavior. He warns them he will send a battalion to fight if they don't stop their nonsense. They're making him mad (figuratively although he does literally go mad after the war). The first colonist is then killed by a British soldier.

This impacts Hamilton's success because the war gives him a chance to improve his position in society, even if how he actually does this is not in the way he intended. He writes instead of fights.

Threatened to Attacked

4. The Scene Event Synthesis: What Story Event sums up the scene's on-the-surface actions, essential above-the-surface worldview behavioral tactics, and beyond-the-surface value change? We will enter that event in the Story Grid Spreadsheet.

King George III sends a "love letter" to the colonists about what will happen if they continue to resist him and then orders British soldiers to kill colonists who disobey.

HOW THE SCENE ABIDES BY THE FIVE COMMANDMENTS OF STORYTELLING

Inciting Incident: Causal. (In Medias Res) King George III sends the colonists a message, warning the colonists that if they push him too hard, he will send his army.

Turning Point Progressive Complication: Active. Off stage, it's presumed they push.

Crisis: Best bad choice. The king can allow the colonies to break from the British reign peacefully, or he can go to war with them.

Climax: The king pledges to kill the colonists' "friends and family." British soldiers turn violent and one shoots and kills a rebel—the beginning of many.

Resolution: The colonies go to war with Great Britain.

- Although not the main antagonist of the story, King George III poses a very real threat to the colonists'—and Hamilton's—survival. The king fulfills the role of dominating antagonist in two of *Hamilton*'s external genre subplots, Society (Historical) and War. These are wonderful subplots for a Status tale, and a lot is packed into this short scene!
- A Society subplot involves a shift in power through rebellion. We have a group of relatively weak underrepresented protagonists striving to overcome a strong tyrant. They have already threatened the reigning power, and in this scene the king delivers a "speech in praise" of the tyrant. This shows us two important elements of the Society story. The power divide between the parties is large (disorganized colonists versus the professional army and navy of a global superpower). We also learn the king's point or why he's engaged in the conflict. The colonies belong to him. He won't give them up and is willing to sacrifice their lives to maintain his property. "You'll Be Back" exemplifies a massive threat encased in humor.
- Most War stories explore brotherhood and a fight for heroic victory to preserve a tribe, nation, or way of life. The revolution is inevitable, and without a war, Hamilton might struggle to rise in status. The war gives Hamilton and the colonists positive and negative consequences—an opportunity but also life-and-death stakes. At the end of this scene, a rebel is killed by the king's soldiers. The war has begun.

"RIGHT HAND MAN"

SCENE 7

SUMMARY

The scene opens to British Admiral Howe arriving with thirty-two thousand troops in New York Harbor. Hamilton, Burr, Laurens, Mulligan, and Lafayette realize this is the opportunity they need to "rise up" and prove themselves.

Washington and his troops struggle to overpower the British. Drowned in paperwork, Washington realizes he needs support if he's going to defeat an army that clearly possesses more weapons and ammunition as well as better-prepared soldiers. His soldiers retreat so any ground gained is lost. Meanwhile, Hamilton goes cannon-stealing with Mulligan.

Burr answers Washington's call for assistance but is quickly dismissed when Hamilton arrives. Washington knows Hamilton turned down positions as secretary with Nathanael Green and Henry Knox but tells Hamilton that wars are won by more than heroic martyrs. "Dying is easy, young man. Living is harder." In other words, it is harder to do the hard work of going on than to jump into the fray and die. Washington asks Hamilton to be his right-hand man, a role that requires doing paperwork and acting as a personal assistant and confidant in planning.

In the background, the company reminds Hamilton not to throw away his shot, which Hamilton acknowledges by accepting the job. He immediately dives into offering suggestions and plans to aid Washington's efforts.

***

ANALYZING THE SCENE

***

STORY EVENT

A Story Event is an active change of a universal human value for one or more characters as a result of conflict (one character's desires clash with another's, or an environmental shift changes the value positively or negatively).

A Working Scene contains at least one Story Event. To determine a scene's Story Event, answer these four Socratic questions:

1. What are the characters literally doing—that is, what are their micro on-the-surface actions?

George Washington and the colonists fight the British.

2. What is the essential tactic of the characters—that is, what above-the-surface macro behaviors are they employing that are linked to a universal human value?

Hamilton wants to attain a higher status, ideally, as a commander in the war or by dying as a martyr. Washington wants to find someone to help him run the war, specifically someone to manage paperwork and be his confidant. To do this, Washington summons Hamilton to his office and offers him a job that requires managing Washington's paperwork and working as his confidant.

3. What beyond-the-surface universal human values have changed for one or more characters in the scene? Which one of those value changes is most important and should be included in the Story Grid Spreadsheet?

Hamilton starts the war as someone with no significant place in society. As the colonies lose battles, he steals British cannons with Mulligan, which catches Washington's attention. Washington asks Hamilton to be his right-hand man and Hamilton accepts, even though this means Hamilton won't be fighting in as many battles. Washington's value shifts from Overwhelmed to Assisted, which impacts Hamilton's success, but to describe this more specifically with reference to Hamilton, we say, he moves from Unknown to Recruited—a big movement toward success.

Unknown to Recruited

4. The Scene Event Synthesis: What Story Event sums up the scene's on-the-surface actions, essential above-the-surface worldview behavioral tactics, and beyond-the-surface value change? We will enter that event in the Story Grid Spreadsheet.

Washington looks for a right-hand man while leading his troops against the thirty-two thousand troops British Admiral Howe commands, and Hamilton agrees.

HOW THE SCENE ABIDES BY THE FIVE COMMANDMENTS OF STORYTELLING

Inciting Incident: Casual. The British invade New York Harbor.

Turning Point Progressive Complication: Active. Washington asks Hamilton to be his right-hand man.

Crisis: Irreconcilable goods choice. Hamilton can reject Washington's offer, or he can accept the offer, even though this means working behind a desk.

Climax: Hamilton accepts Washington's offer and immediately gives advice on how to proceed.

Resolution: Washington is relieved and bolstered, and Hamilton is excited for the opportunity.

NOTES

- The differences in personality between Washington as mentor and Hamilton as apprentice sets up a wonderful dynamic tension between these two key roles in the Status Story. Whether the protagonist listens to and applies the mentor's advice determines the subgenre. Disregarding a mentor's advice is the hallmark of a cautionary story, including the Tragic subgenre. Although Hamilton admires Washington, he doesn't always listen or grasp the full meaning behind Washington's advice. We'll see this more as Hamilton grows increasingly frustrated with his job during the war.
- Don't overlook Washington's dismissal of Burr when Hamilton arrives. This is one of many blows Burr suffers because he chooses to wait and be patient. The rift between Hamilton and Burr grows.
- Hamilton pushes back when Washington tries to understand why he rejected offers to work for Nathanael Green and Henry Knox. Hamilton struggles to contain his anger, even toward Washington, the man he respects most. This personality trait sets up a common pattern that arises before many of Hamilton's biggest mistakes.
- The return of "my shot" in Hamilton's response to Washington ("I'm not throwing away my shot!") pinpoints a moment when Hamilton sets aside his dream of being a martyr to gain success. However, just because Hamilton sacrifices his dream temporarily doesn't mean he forsakes the idea.

- This scene establishes the overwhelming odds faced by the colonists in the War Story subplot.

"A WINTER'S BALL" AND "HELPLESS"

SCENE 8

SUMMARY

"A Winter's Ball" and "Helpless" combine to create one scene. At the beginning, Hamilton has elevated his status by becoming Washington's right-hand man. Burr sets the scene here with spiteful words (his envy masquerading as humor) that spill over into his interaction with Hamilton. He teases Hamilton before the ball that Hamilton would become a rich man if he married a Schuyler sister. Of course, Hamilton responds wittily, "Is it a question of if, Burr, or which one?"

This entertaining banter transitions to "Helpless" where Eliza and her sisters attend the Winter's Ball. Eliza introduces herself as the sister who never tries to "grab the spotlight" (that's Angelica's role), but she feels the need to do so that night. She has spotted Hamilton, and with Angelica's assistance (something we will revisit in the next song), Eliza meets him. Her last name catches his attention, but her compassion, sophistication, and charm secure his genuine affection for her.

Hamilton courts Eliza with love letters. She fears her rich and politically connected father will deny Hamilton's request for marriage. Her fears are unfounded, however. Philip Schuyler agrees to the match with a plea for Eliza and Hamilton to "be true," an important line that foreshadows challenges ahead for the couple.

ANALYZING THE SCENE

STORY EVENT

A Story Event is an active change of a universal human value for one or more characters as a result of conflict (one character's desires clash with another's, or an environmental shift changes the value positively or negatively).

A Working Scene contains at least one Story Event. To determine a scene's Story Event, answer these four Socratic questions:

1. What are the characters literally doing—that is, what are their micro on-the-surface actions?

Hamilton courts Eliza Schuyler.

2. What is the essential tactic of the characters—that is, what above-the-surface macro behaviors are they employing that are linked to a universal human value?

Hamilton wants to find a wife he can love but also to improve his status. Eliza is attracted to Hamilton, but she's not sure Hamilton likes her or if her father will accept her chosen mate.

3. What beyond-the-surface universal human values have changed for one or more characters in the scene? Which one of those value changes is most important and should be included in the Story Grid Spreadsheet?

Hamilton enters the Winter's Ball in search of a rich and/or famous wife, and he's interested in a Schuyler sister. Eliza falls head over heels for Hamilton. She grows more and more vulnerable because of his romantic pursuits. Hamilton asks for Eliza's hand in marriage, and he confesses his fears and vulnerabilities to Eliza. They both remain in this vulnerable state although Hamilton's fear is only ever communicated to his wife.

Unmarried to Married

4. The Scene Event Synthesis: What Story Event sums up the scene's on-the-surface actions, essential above-the-surface worldview behavioral tactics, and beyond-the-surface value change? We will enter that event in the Story Grid Spreadsheet.

Hamilton meets Eliza at a Winter's Ball, and soon they are married.

HOW THE SCENE ABIDES BY THE FIVE COMMANDMENTS OF STORYTELLING

Inciting Incident: Causal. Hamilton walks into the room, and Eliza's "heart goes boom."

Turning Point Progressive Complication: Active. Angelica introduces Hamilton to Eliza.

Crisis: Irreconcilable goods choice. Does Hamilton risk rejection by humbling himself to win over Eliza, or does Hamilton forsake his pursuit of Eliza for another woman?

Climax: Hamilton courts Eliza and asks for her hand in marriage, which she accepts! Hamilton confides in Eliza, sharing his fears and vulnerabilities, and momentarily considers a quieter life as her husband.

Resolution: Eliza and Hamilton get married.

NOTES

- This scene has more than one Crisis, which often happens

when a scene delivers the obligatory moments of a Love Story subplot. Eliza's Crisis is similar to Hamilton's. Does she accept Hamilton's courtship at risk of being forever "helpless," or try to forget about him, despite believing she'll probably never find a man she could love as much. How do we determine which Crisis is most important? We look at the climactic action that resolves the central question in the scene, especially when they enhance Hamilton's success. Marrying into a wealthy and connected family does that for Hamilton.

- What's the big takeaway from this scene? Hamilton hesitates in his desire for status and ambition—though briefly—for a newfound chance at peace and serenity with Eliza. They get married, elevating Hamilton's financial status.

- While gaining some considerable financial advantage, Hamilton also admits that he has fears and vulnerabilities after gaining permission to wed. We don't get this a lot from Hamilton. In fact, Eliza is the only character he talks to about this. This is a testament to his genuine affection for Eliza, even if he does engage in emotional and physical affairs later in the story. We gain sympathy for Hamilton and are witnesses to their intimacy with one another despite their future marital hardships.

- Hamilton and Eliza's love story is a perfect example of two lovers who are unequal in status, which complicates their relationship because they have different wants and needs. Although they weren't a politically and socially "right" match, Eliza, full of grace and compassion, sees much more in Hamilton than his ambitions. This is a testament to her genuine character, and a major reason we all love her. This is also a stupendous setup for her saving Hamilton's legacy despite his mistakes.

- Angelica introduces Hamilton to Eliza, which is brought to our attention in the following scene. Here, we see this action as nothing more than an older sister playing Eliza's "wingwoman." In reality, this is a sacrifice that alters the course of Angelica's life—a major setup to be paid off.

- **Fun Fact:** Hamilton and Eliza really did exchange love letters during their courtship. In one, Hamilton expresses his undying love for Eliza with a short poem.[1] Eliza wore this love poem in a necklace for the rest of her life (fifty years *after* Hamilton was shot and killed in the infamous duel). How can we *not* adore Eliza? Normally, a character who seems too perfect is a problem.[2] This is something Miranda and Ron Chernow (author of *Alexander Hamilton*, the inspiration for *Hamilton*) discussed during the musical adaptation. And yet "Helpless" shows Eliza is a complex character. Her vulnerability is a challenge that gives her strength and reinforces her determination and compassion. This also suggests Eliza's story arc is one of Status Admiration and will end prescriptively despite Hamilton's death and inability to know for sure if she preserves Hamilton's legacy.

---

1. You can see this poem in Miranda and McCarter, *Hamilton: The Revolution*, 69.
2. Miranda and McCarter, *Hamilton: The Revolution*, 107.

"SATISFIED"
SCENE 9

SUMMARY

At Hamilton and Eliza's wedding reception, Angelica is delivering a toast when the word "satisfied" causes her to go back in time to when she and Eliza first met Hamilton at the Winter's Ball.

Angelica is attracted to Hamilton right away and recognizes him as a kindred spirit, but when she learns Eliza is interested in him, she decides to introduce them for reasons she fully understands. Angelica can't marry Hamilton because of her position in her family, and though she would rather be his partner, allowing him to meet (and marry) Eliza paves the way to have this intelligent and worthy man in her life.

We return to the wedding reception in the present, where Angelica considers that she is still attracted to Hamilton and that neither will be satisfied with their circumstances. Left unsaid are the potential consequences of Hamilton's inability to be satisfied in his life.

ANALYZING THE SCENE

STORY EVENT

A Story Event is an active change of a universal human value for one or more characters as a result of conflict (one character's desires clash with another's, or an environmental shift changes the value positively or negatively).

A Working Scene contains at least one Story Event. To determine a scene's Story Event, answer these four Socratic questions:

1. What are the characters literally doing—that is, what are their micro on-the-surface actions?

While offering a toast to Alexander and Eliza at their wedding, Angelica reflects on the night she and Eliza met Hamilton.

2. What is the essential tactic of the characters—that is, what above-the-surface macro behaviors are they employing that are linked to a universal human value?

Angelica wants Eliza and Hamilton to be happy, but she loves Hamilton and also wants him as her romantic partner. She wants satisfaction in life but knows she will never have it. Her revelation of the three fundamental truths reinforces this.

3. What beyond-the-surface universal human values have changed for one or more characters in the scene? Which one of those value changes is most important and should be included in the Story Grid Spreadsheet?

Hamilton and Eliza are married, and Angelica begins the scene happy with a toast to the newlyweds. The scene rewinds to the night she and Eliza met Hamilton when Angelica sacrificed a potential romantic relationship with him in favor of her sister. After reviewing her memories, she is left with the conclusion that she and Hamilton will never be content. Hamilton moves from poor to rich because he marries into a wealthy family, but what's significant is that Hamilton's marriage is made possible because Angelica gave up her shot.

Happy for the Newlyweds to Protective of Her Sister

4. The Scene Event Synthesis: What Story Event sums up the scene's on-the-surface actions, essential above-the-surface worldview behavioral tactics, and beyond-the-surface value change? We will enter that event in the Story Grid Spreadsheet.

Angelica toasts Hamilton and Eliza at their wedding while reminiscing about the night she met Hamilton and the life she sacrificed for her sister, making this marriage and another rise in Hamilton's status possible.

HOW THE SCENE ABIDES BY THE FIVE COMMANDMENTS OF STORYTELLING

Inciting Incident: Causal. Angelica offers a toast at Eliza and Alexander's wedding.

Turning Point Progressive Complication: Revelatory. Angelica realizes Hamilton's inability to be satisfied could end up hurting Eliza.

Crisis: Best bad choice. Angelica can remain silent about this insight, or she can warn Hamilton or Eliza while risking alienation and her sister's happiness.

Climax: Angelica toasts Hamilton and Eliza's marriage, deciding to not speak up about her concerns about him. Better to keep them both in her life than to risk offense.

Resolution: Angelica knows she and Hamilton will never be satisfied. Angelica does keep Hamilton in her life.

NOTES

- "Satisfied" foreshadows Washington's warning without

quoting his words. The facts of history change depending on who tells the story, and Hamilton and Angelica flirtatiously and unapologetically attract one another. It also unveils Angelica's greatest sacrifice. She gives up Hamilton for Eliza. This selfless decision, perfectly juxtaposed against her decision to remain dissatisfied forever, proves Angelica's ultimate object of desire and utmost love for her sister. She will do anything for Eliza, which illustrates an important characteristic reinforced by her actions.

- Raise a glass to the power of point of view! Seeing the Winter's Ball again from Angelica's viewpoint helps us see a different side of Hamilton and understand the sacrifice Angelica makes, resulting in frustration and heartbreak. She admits she may have been too quick in sizing up Hamilton. And what a selfless thing to do—to give up Hamilton to Eliza—despite the reality that it doomed her to a life of dissatisfaction. She's an important narrator later in the story, and this scene lends her credibility. (Don't discount the role sympathy plays in how much we trust what a character tells us.)

- It's important to remember that Angelica met Hamilton before Eliza, which is why the flashback rewinds all the way to their meeting. Angelica had all the power in their exchange, and Hamilton confirms this when he giddily encourages her to "Lead the way!" It probably shocked Hamilton when she introduced him to Eliza, but notice his sincere attraction to Eliza, too. He wasn't without love for Eliza even if he was attracted to Angelica's intellect.

- Miranda admits Philip Schuyler did have sons and Angelica was already married, contrary to what Angelica says in the lyrics. Writers of historical fiction often have to adjust the facts to "serve a larger point."[1] Historically and in the story, Angelica is attracted to Hamilton (their letters suggest this was mutual), and she knows she can't have him. This personal introduction sets up Angelica's role later, provides a rival (Love Story convention), and makes the "Lovers Meet" scene (Love Story obligatory moment) more engaging.

- Notice the change in tone in Hamilton's voice when Eliza says her last name. Angelica was right in her thought that Alexander was first attracted to her because she is a Schuyler sister. Novelists don't have the benefit of talented actors to do this for us. What other tools can we use to convey this without sound?

- Miranda is particularly skilled at word play, and he needs to be to tell a story in the form of a musical. The actors and music provide dramatic advantages, but the medium constrains the number of words the writer can use. Each one must do more than one thing. Using words like "helpless," "satisfied," and "my shot" is smart because they have multiple meanings even within the same context.[2] When a writer is this intentional with their craft, it's worth it to examine the work closely whether we're analyzing the story in a high school English class or as a professional writer.

---

1. McCarter and Miranda, *Hamilton: The Revolution*, 83n9.
2. McCarter and Miranda, *Hamilton: The Revolution*, 80n3.

"THE STORY OF TONIGHT" (REPRISE)
SCENE 10

SUMMARY

The reprise of "The Story of Tonight" checks in on Hamilton and his companions after the wedding when Burr arrives to congratulate Hamilton on his marriage. Tension spikes between Burr and the three friends.

Laurens, Mulligan, and Lafayette take a jab at Burr while Hamilton congratulates him on his promotion to lieutenant colonel. They discuss the merits of their current positions. Hamilton would rather be fighting Washington's battles than managing his correspondence. Laurens interjects that he's heard Burr has a woman on the side. Hamilton congratulates Burr on the relationship, but Burr confesses he can't pursue her. "She's married to a British officer."

Hamilton experiences a revelation that deepens his misunderstanding of Burr's character. Burr is in love but won't act on it—something Hamilton would never do.

The scene ends with the men walking in opposite directions, emphasizing their opposing points of view—a dynamic that will drive their relationship, decisions, and behavior for the remainder of the story.

ANALYZING THE SCENE

STORY EVENT

A Story Event is an active change of a universal human value for one or more characters as a result of conflict (one character's desires clash with another's, or an environmental shift changes the value positively or negatively).

A Working Scene contains at least one Story Event. To determine a scene's Story Event, answer these four Socratic questions:

1. What are the characters literally doing—that is, what are their micro on-the-surface actions?

Hamilton enjoys drinks with his buddies when Burr comes to congratulate him.

2. What is the essential tactic of the characters—that is, what above-the-surface macro behaviors are they employing that are linked to a universal human value?

Hamilton wants Burr to take control of his life. Burr wants glory to come to him through steadfast self-control and patience. The essential tactic is Hamilton's wish that Burr would take action. We can almost see Hamilton thinking, "How can this man be my friend and do nothing?"

3. What beyond-the-surface universal human values have changed for one or more characters in the scene? Which one of those value changes is most important and should be included in the Story Grid Spreadsheet?

Although pleased with his marriage, Hamilton longs for what he doesn't have, even to the point that his yearning blinds him to his great advantage. After Hamilton learns of Burr's refusal to "get" Theodosia, his respect for Burr turns. It's clear they are very different men in how they act—even if Hamilton likes Burr as a person. This reaffirms how Burr will not help Hamilton rise to success, and Hamilton knows this.

Close to Growing Distant

4. The Scene Event Synthesis: What Story Event sums up the scene's on-the-surface actions, essential above-the-surface worldview behavioral tactics, and beyond-the-surface value change? We will enter that event in the Story Grid Spreadsheet.

A wedge is driven between the two friends because Hamilton can't understand why Burr is willing to wait for the woman he loves.

HOW THE SCENE ABIDES BY THE FIVE COMMANDMENTS OF STORYTELLING

Inciting Incident: Causal. Burr visits Hamilton at the bar to congratulate him on his marriage.

Turning Point Progressive Complication: Revelatory. Hamilton learns that Burr's woman is married, so Burr won't publicly pursue her.

Crisis: Irreconcilable goods choice. Hamilton can either support Burr and his decision to wait until Theodosia is available, or he can encourage Burr to "go get her."

Climax: Hamilton tells Burr that he doesn't understand him and encourages Burr to pursue the relationship.

Resolution: Hamilton and Burr leave as friends, but their differences are pushing them away from one another.

NOTES

- Unlike the first appearance of this song, this reprise serves as a complete scene because Burr arrives on set, setting the Five Commandments in motion and causing a value shift that affects Hamilton's movement toward success.
- Burr has come to congratulate Hamilton on his marriage, and tension spikes between Burr and the three friends as it did in the earlier version of the song. Can you see how repeating similar scenes with similar conflicts and setting can show change over time? The circumstances must be different enough, so it doesn't feel like we're going over the same territory, but this scene gives us an opportunity to take stock of the state of this vital relationship. Hamilton isn't simply disagreeing with Burr on a point of policy (should the colonies go to war or not) but with his temperament and approach to life.
- Ultimately, this scene portrays a group of four buddies singing about their hopes and dreams. The lyrics reveal their innocence and aspirations to be and do more than they are in the present as well as the hope that they will achieve greatness together. They dream of glory, even if death should take them before they live to see it. Their focus is on legacy—the essence of success (and Status as a Global Genre).
- Hamilton and Burr circle each other for the entirety of Hamilton's adult life, yet with backgrounds more similar than not, Hamilton and Burr's dwindling relationship speaks to one reason the musical has become a cultural phenomenon. The protagonist and antagonist want the same object of desire—success—but the way they define it and how they pursue it creates conflict that causes two friends to end as foes. We're hooked!
- Notice how the external subplots—War, Performance, Society, and Love—aren't driving the major change in *Hamilton*, but they create external circumstances that constantly force Hamilton and his main antagonist, Burr, to consider the way they define success. They both struggle

with the needs underlying these genres—security, esteem, recognition, and connection respectively. How they react to their external circumstances defines these characters and affects their relationship for the worse.

"WAIT FOR IT"

SCENE 11

SUMMARY

After the argument with Hamilton, Burr stands alone and contemplates his current crisis and whether his general approach is the right one. Does he share his beliefs and risk everything or keep quiet and hope his reputation is saved?

Burr believes Hamilton can take bold action because he has nothing to lose. But Burr has his reputation, wealth, and Theodosia to protect. Hamilton has gained success, but many men who have taken similar risks in the revolution have died. Burr knows he can die no matter what his intentions are, and even if he acts out of justice, doing so rashly will likely lead to destruction and disaster.

Burr decides to keep waiting for his rewards to give himself the best chance in the future.

ANALYZING THE SCENE

STORY EVENT

A Story Event is an active change of a universal human value for one or more characters as a result of conflict (one character's desires clash with another's, or an environmental shift changes the value positively or negatively).

A Working Scene contains at least one Story Event. To determine a scene's Story Event, answer these four Socratic questions:

1. What are the characters literally doing—that is, what are their micro on-the-surface actions?

Burr contemplates whether he is doing the right thing by waiting for Theodosia (and in general).

2. What is the essential tactic of the characters—that is, what above-the-surface macro behaviors are they employing that are linked to a universal human value?

Burr wants success and to be with Theodosia, but he fears acting too soon will result in negative consequences. He debates how he should behave to be successful, and he concludes that living by his motto is his best chance.

3. What beyond-the-surface universal human values have changed for one or more characters in the scene? Which one of those value changes is most important and should be included in the Story Grid Spreadsheet?

In the prior scene Hamilton challenges Burr's decision to wait for Theodosia. Burr considers Hamilton's success but then justifies his own motive for waiting. Others who follow Hamilton's course have died. Burr is confident in his choice, even if he can't understand how Hamilton can act rashly and be rewarded.
Doubting to Confident

4. The Scene Event Synthesis: What Story Event sums up the scene's on-the-surface actions, essential above-the-surface worldview behavioral tactics, and beyond-the-surface value change? We will enter that event in the Story Grid Spreadsheet.

After Hamilton's confrontation about Theodosia, Burr questions his approach to success but concludes that waiting is the best course.

HOW THE SCENE ABIDES BY THE FIVE COMMANDMENTS OF STORYTELLING

Inciting Incident: Causal. Hamilton criticizes Burr's decision to wait.

Turning Point Progressive Complication: Revelatory. Burr recognizes that he's still alive when so many others who acted out have died. He thinks there must be a reason for this.

Crisis: Best bad choice. Burr can act like Hamilton by taking risks without worrying about consequences in hope of getting ahead, or Burr can continue to work hard and wait patiently for his efforts to pay off.

Climax: Burr defends his decision to wait. He will keep his relationship with Theodosia private until the time is better for them to go public.

Resolution: Meanwhile, he observes Hamilton's climb to success from afar.

NOTES

- Our sympathy for Burr to a large extent comes from the secrets he reveals in this scene. Up to this point, the audience understands that Burr wants success like Hamilton, but we have no idea why Burr hesitates to pursue what he wants. Here we learn he has a point.
- All of us know what it's like to experience the consequences

of our decisions and joys when we move toward what we want to achieve. While Burr is the epitome of a Status character who sells out, "Wait for It" shows us why.

- This song touches on very human fears and rationalizations that prevent us from moving forward. We don't want to lose what we already have. Like Hamilton, we might disagree with Burr's approach, but unlike Hamilton, we now have the benefit of understanding Burr's motives. We can sympathize with his situation, the decisions he makes, the burdens he bears, and the growing jealousy that skyrockets to an all-time high when we reach the story's Climax.

"STAY ALIVE"

SCENE 12

SUMMARY

Hamilton's blissful and quiet life in suburbia is quickly uprooted by the Revolutionary War but not in the way he would prefer. His repeated requests to fight on the field are denied. The colonial army is at a disadvantage and a change in tactics is in order. Washington realizes they must go on the offensive, but that doesn't include employing Hamilton on the field.

When Washington promotes Charles Lee to the position of general, we taste Hamilton's spite. "He's not the choice I would have gone with." Hamilton is right. Lee fails miserably in the Battle of Monmouth.

Disgusted with Lee's cowardice, Washington directs Hamilton to put Lafayette in charge. Left behind, Lee badmouths Washington. Hamilton and Laurens don't want to tolerate the insult, but Washington forbids retribution. Hamilton respects Washington (his mentor) enough to not *directly* disobey Washington's orders. Laurens steps up to duel Lee instead, and Hamilton agrees to be Laurens' second.

ANALYZING THE SCENE

57

STORY EVENT

A Story Event is an active change of a universal human value for one or more characters as a result of conflict (one character's desires clash with another's, or an environmental shift changes the value positively or negatively).

A Working Scene contains at least one Story Event. To determine a scene's Story Event, answer these four Socratic questions:

1. What are the characters literally doing—that is, what are their micro on-the-surface actions?

Hamilton writes essays and letters while Washington and the other soldiers fight in the Revolutionary War.

2. What is the essential tactic of the characters—that is, what above-the-surface macro behaviors are they employing that are linked to a universal human value?

Hamilton wants to fight, not participate from behind a desk. Washington refuses this because he won't risk losing Hamilton's mind. Washington appoints Charles Lee as commander instead. Later, Laurens wants Lee to pay for badmouthing Washington and demands he and Hamilton do something to stop Lee.

3. What beyond-the-surface universal human values have changed for one or more characters in the scene? Which one of those value changes is most important and should be included in the Story Grid Spreadsheet?

Despite his frustration, Hamilton remains obedient to Washington. He requests command of a battalion but consistently returns to his desk when instructed. Washington appoints Lee to command, which leads to a major defeat and the deaths of many men. He was promoted but then is demoted. When Lee badmouths Washington, Laurens and Hamilton demand Lee pay for it. Hamilton won't act directly against Washington's orders, but he will support Laurens.

Obedient to Disobedient

4. The Scene Event Synthesis: What Story Event sums up the scene's on-the-surface actions, essential above-the-surface worldview behavioral tactics, and beyond-the-surface value change? We will enter that event in the Story Grid Spreadsheet.

Washington appoints Lee to command at the Battle of Monmouth. When he fails and badmouths Washington, Hamilton indirectly disobeys Washington's orders not to retaliate.

HOW THE SCENE ABIDES BY THE FIVE COMMANDMENTS OF STORYTELLING

Inciting Incident: Causal. Washington is discouraged by the progress of the war, and the Continental Congress is pressing for results.

Turning Point Progressive Complication: Active. Charles Lee badmouths Washington after Washington demotes him.

Crisis: Best bad choice. Hamilton can speak out against Washington's instructions, or he can remain obedient to the general's wishes.

Climax: Hamilton obeys the letter of Washington's instructions.

Resolution: Laurens calls a duel against Lee, and Hamilton tells Laurens he will be his second.

NOTES

- At the beginning of this scene, Hamilton is still, sitting at a desk and writing, but his mind is racing. He notices Washington's low spirits and defends the general's tactics by emphasizing the lack of resources. The colonies are at an extreme disadvantage, a reality that Washington and Hamilton discuss. They agree that the only way to defeat the British is to go on the offensive and "Make it impossible [for the king] to justify the cost of the fight." But they disagree on how to implement this strategy.

- Notice multiple important Crisis questions are in this scene. Washington once more denies Hamilton's request to fight but under different circumstances and with greater stakes. (This is the key to avoiding boring scenes when the characters behave consistently.) Washington can give Lee (or someone else) command and further agitate Hamilton, or he can appoint Hamilton as general. Washington probably doesn't want to frustrate Hamilton, but he can't justify risking Hamilton's life and losing his brilliant mind. In this way, Washington suffers a best bad choice. It makes sense to track Hamilton's point of view in this scene because he is the main protagonist and his decision impacts the global value the most.

- Washington gives command to Lee, and Hamilton's debate about whether to listen is evident when Hamilton says he can't disobey "direct orders." But that doesn't keep Hamilton from finding a loophole in the instructions and acting as Laurens' second in the next scene.

- Once again, we see the importance of the role between protagonist and mentor in a Status Story. Washington seeks to help Hamilton, despite his aggravation of constantly being denied command. In cautionary Status stories, the protagonist eventually foregoes the mentor's instruction and/or wisdom. Washington is a man of prominence and patience, a man of resolute command and steady grace. While Hamilton respects this, he doesn't always listen to Washington's instructions (especially when he's not physically present).

"TEN DUEL COMMANDMENTS"
SCENE 13

SUMMARY

Hamilton and Burr narrate this scene in which we learn through the ten commandments of dueling how these events proceed. When the conflict can't be worked out through other means, a date, time, and location are chosen, and the participants prepare for the worst. Burr and Hamilton act as the designated seconds. This is the final opportunity to prevent the duel.

Burr says, "Duels are dumb and immature," and while Hamilton agrees, he believes Lee should not get away with badmouthing Washington. Burr realizes Hamilton and Laurens won't back down.

The duel commences, and Laurens shoots first, striking Lee clean in his side.

ANALYZING THE SCENE

STORY EVENT

A Story Event is an active change of a universal human value for one or more characters as a result of conflict (one character's desires clash with another's, or an environmental shift changes the value positively or negatively).

A Working Scene contains at least one Story Event. To determine a scene's Story Event, answer these four Socratic questions:

1. What are the characters literally doing—that is, what are their micro on-the-surface actions?

Hamilton and Burr discuss details, and then Laurens and Lee duel.

2. What is the essential tactic of the characters—that is, what above-the-surface macro behaviors are they employing that are linked to a universal human value?

Hamilton and Laurens want Lee to pay for his bad behavior. Lee wants to blame Washington for his disaster, and Burr wants to negotiate a more peaceful and logical resolution for Lee's actions.

3. What beyond-the-surface universal human values have changed for one or more characters in the scene? Which one of those value changes is most important and should be included in the Story Grid Spreadsheet?

Hamilton and Burr accept positions as Laurens' and Lee's seconds. The four, and a doctor, walk through the ten commandments, leading up to commandment eight, when Hamilton and Burr meet to negotiate. Hamilton refuses to accept Burr's negotiations, and the duel proceeds. Laurens shoots Lee in the side, winning the duel. Hamilton is pleased with the result and doesn't realize his decision to participate will anger his mentor.

Furious to Pleased

4. The Scene Event Synthesis: What Story Event sums up the scene's on-the-surface actions, essential above-the-surface worldview

behavioral tactics, and beyond-the-surface value change? We will enter that event in the Story Grid Spreadsheet.

After negotiations between Hamilton and Burr break down, the duel commences, and Laurens shoots Lee.

HOW THE SCENE ABIDES BY THE FIVE COMMANDMENTS OF STORYTELLING

Inciting Incident: Causal. Hamilton accepts the role as Laurens' second.

Turning Point Progressive Complication: Active. Hamilton meets Burr and agrees that duels are immature and nonsensical, but Lee won't apologize.

Crisis: Best bad choice. Hamilton can negotiate with Burr to stop the duel even if Lee won't admit he was wrong and ask for forgiveness, or he can allow the duel to go forward.

Climax: No accommodation can be reached, so Laurens and Lee proceed with the duel.

Resolution: Laurens shoots Lee in the side. Hamilton celebrates their win, and Laurens says he's satisfied.

NOTES

- This is another scene with multiple clear Crisis questions. Burr can try to convince Lee to admit to his wrongs and ask for forgiveness, or he can allow the duel to proceed.
- Miranda explains that Burr wasn't actually Lee's second in this duel because at this time he opposed them generally.[1] Notice the smart choice to adapt the event in this scene. Isn't it more intense because the protagonist and antagonist are on opposite sides of this conflict here? Although not facing

each other directly, these friends are becoming frenemies, a divide that only grows. Substituting Burr here allows Miranda to show this process unfolding gradually.

- Dramatizing the structure and process of a typical duel allows the audience to see and accept this was not an unusual way to resolve individual conflicts at this time. Isn't the war between Britain and the American Colonies similar on a larger scale?

---

1. McCarter and Miranda, *Hamilton: The Revolution*, 100n3.

"MEET ME INSIDE"

SCENE 14

SUMMARY

After Laurens wins the duel, a furious Washington arrives to scold Hamilton for his foolishness. The general commands him to "meet me inside."

In private, Washington refers to Hamilton as "son" and explains why he doesn't want Hamilton on the battlefield. Washington can't risk losing his brilliant mind in battle, but he also cares about Hamilton and wants to keep him alive.

Washington's explanation, however, falls on deaf ears. With each repetition of "son," Hamilton erupts with obvious and growing frustration. He snaps at Washington, "I'm not your son."

Eventually, Hamilton crosses the line by shouting. Washington commands him to go home and dismisses him when Hamilton pleads.

ANALYZING THE SCENE

STORY EVENT

A Story Event is an active change of a universal human value for one or more characters as a result of conflict (one character's desires clash with another's, or an environmental shift changes the value positively or negatively).

A Working Scene contains at least one Story Event. To determine a scene's Story Event, answer these four Socratic questions:

1. What are the characters literally doing—that is, what are their micro on-the-surface actions?

Washington lectures Hamilton on his dangerous and inappropriate behavior.

2. What is the essential tactic of the characters—that is, what above-the-surface macro behaviors are they employing that are linked to a universal human value?

Washington wants to keep Hamilton safe. Hamilton has no concern for his safety and wants to command a battalion. While Washington tries to reason with him, Hamilton shouts at his mentor.

3. What beyond-the-surface universal human values have changed for one or more characters in the scene? Which one of those value changes is most important and should be included in the Story Grid Spreadsheet?

Washington's request to speak in private humiliates Hamilton. The two argue, leading to Hamilton's outburst, which crosses a line. Washington sends Hamilton home.

Triumphant to Failure

4. The Scene Event Synthesis: What Story Event sums up the scene's on-the-surface actions, essential above-the-surface worldview behavioral tactics, and beyond-the-surface value

change? We will enter that event in the Story Grid
Spreadsheet.

*Washington scolds Hamilton for his participation in the duel and sends
him home.*

HOW THE SCENE ABIDES BY THE FIVE COMMANDMENTS OF STORYTELLING

Inciting Incident: Causal. Washington orders Hamilton to speak with
him privately.

Turning Point Progressive Complication: Active. Hamilton speaks out
against Washington in a way that crosses a line. It's a final straw for
both of them.

Crisis: Best bad choice. Washington can accept Hamilton's outburst
and give him a battalion to command at the risk of Hamilton never
learning his place and/or dying. Or, Washington can send Hamilton
home, giving him a chance to cool off while guaranteeing his safety.

Climax: Washington commands Hamilton to go home to Eliza. "That's
an order from your commander."

Resolution: Disappointed, Hamilton returns home.

NOTES

- Although Hamilton starts the scene high, he ends extremely
  low. Before, Hamilton was kept behind the scenes during the
  Revolutionary War. Now he's been sent home.
- A key component of a cautionary Status Story is a
  protagonist who fails to heed a mentor's guidance. While
  Hamilton often listens to Washington, his defiance
  foreshadows Hamilton's habit of forgetting that "history has
  its eyes on him," some wisdom he will hear from

67

Washington later in the war. Hamilton's focus on third-party validation is a danger to himself and others.

- When Washington refers to Hamilton as "son" in this scene, we get the feeling he cares about Hamilton, doesn't want to see him hurt, and can't risk losing him. Hamilton, however, remains defiant and doesn't care about his safety. He is so focused on what he wants—to acquire command in the war —that he can't see Washington's point. Instead, he dismisses his mentor's wisdom and argues. Which, as we see, backfires.

"THAT WOULD BE ENOUGH"

SCENE 15

SUMMARY

After being dismissed, Hamilton returns home feeling disgruntled and disappointed. Eliza greets him and tells him she's pregnant.

Shocked, elated, and horrified, Hamilton insists Eliza should have told him. Eliza shares how she wrote to Washington, begging him to send Hamilton home. This is a revelation because Eliza's letters would have added to Washington's concern for Hamilton's safety.

Hamilton worries whether he'll be able to support his family, but Eliza urges him to recognize how fortunate they are that he has survived and they are together as a family.

Eliza accepts Hamilton for who he is, no matter his success or wealth, though she supports his ambitions. Eliza's definition of success differs from his, and she believes as long as he returns to his her once his work is done, she will be content. She tells him, "That would be enough."

Hamilton kisses her hand. For a fleeting moment, he accepts and respects her wishes.

ANALYZING THE SCENE

_____

STORY EVENT

A Story Event is an active change of a universal human value for one or more characters as a result of conflict (one character's desires clash with another's, or an environmental shift changes the value positively or negatively).

A Working Scene contains at least one Story Event. To determine a scene's Story Event, answer these four Socratic questions:

1. What are the characters literally doing—that is, what are their micro on-the-surface actions?

Eliza and Hamilton are reunited, and she shares news of her pregnancy and her vision for the kind of marriage and life she wants with him.

2. What is the essential tactic of the characters—that is, what above-the-surface macro behaviors are they employing that are linked to a universal human value?

Hamilton wants to create a legacy. He believes this is possible if he is a rich and important man who can provide for his wife and children and who contributes to forging the new nation. Being a part of Hamilton's life is enough for Eliza, but she also supports his professional endeavors if he comes home at the end of the day and opens his heart to her. Hamilton starts to listen.

3. What beyond-the-surface universal human values have changed for one or more characters in the scene? Which one of those value changes is most important and should be included in the Story Grid Spreadsheet?

Hamilton returns home ashamed and disappointed. Eliza, however, welcomes him with open arms. She's pregnant, which thrills and troubles Hamilton. How can Eliza relish being a "poor man's wife"? Eliza explains that she doesn't care about his legacy or status in society. She just wants to be a part of Hamilton's "narrative" no matter what it is. Hamilton accepts this, kisses her hand, and momentarily finds peace in her quiet courage and humility. Eliza begins as an outsider in Hamilton's professional life and ends as part of his life while Hamilton begins disappointed and ends humbled despite feeling unsatisfied.

Ashamed to Humbled

4. The Scene Event Synthesis: What Story Event sums up the scene's on-the-surface actions, essential above-the-surface worldview behavioral tactics, and beyond-the-surface value change? We will enter that event in the Story Grid Spreadsheet.

Hamilton returns home to a pregnant Eliza who tries to convince him that they don't need money or a legacy to live happily.

HOW THE SCENE ABIDES BY THE FIVE COMMANDMENTS OF STORYTELLING

Inciting Incident: Causal. Hamilton comes home to a pregnant Eliza.

Turning Point Progressive Complication: Active. Eliza asks Hamilton to let her be a part of his narrative.

Crisis: Irreconcilable goods choice. Hamilton can believe that all they need for success in life is each other or not.

Climax: For a brief moment in the story, Hamilton accepts Eliza's good but unambitious dream of a simple life, motivated by love instead of glory. Hamilton kisses Eliza's hand and they quietly spend the night together.

Resolution: Hamilton momentarily flirts with the idea of focusing on family over what he originally valued as a legacy worth telling (based on professional success).

NOTES

- In the context of the genre, Hamilton's relentless pride and ambition push him up and down the global Status value gradient from Selling Out to Success. His refusal to give up his pride brings his destruction. "That Would Be Enough" marks one of the few moments when Hamilton puts his relationship with Eliza above his ambition. Though he finds the idea of being poor unsatisfying, this moment plants seeds for life and hope.
- We see in this song how Eliza challenges Hamilton's worldview, a necessary component of Story Grid's Heroic Journey 2.0. He is temporarily enlightened. Hamilton wants to be there for Eliza, but over time he fails to see and hold on to what Eliza understands all along. They don't need success, money, or a legacy to be happy and fulfilled. His inability to accept this truth is a clear sign of a cautionary Status tale. Hamilton's moments of clarity and maturity often shift backward when opportunities that could grant him his version of success appear.
- Why offer hope when we know from the opening scene that Hamilton doesn't survive? A story that incorporates the Heroic Journey 2.0, even if it's a cautionary tale, should offer clues about the path that avoids tragedy. We can see the places where Hamilton makes positive progress as well as where he goes astray. Dramatic irony ensures we can recognize these moments as we encounter them. Incidentally, this works because in the opening scene Miranda generates empathy by showing us what Hamilton wants and why.
- Multiple characters in a Status Story can fill the role of mentor. Washington is Hamilton's professional mentor, but that doesn't mean Eliza doesn't also offer mentorship. Again,

a mentor is a chaotic force that upsets the protagonist's life to encourage them to grow or realize their potential. Eliza's insistence that family life could be enough is a different but important call to adventure.

- Don't mistake Eliza's simple desires in life (especially when compared to Angelica's) as characteristics of a weak and subordinate female character. Again, there is strength in vulnerability and the ability to forgive. By embracing and celebrating the Platonic ideals of truth, beauty, and goodness, Eliza personifies these virtues. This is heroic in any period but particularly in a time of war. We think of the American victory as a foregone conclusion, but it was not guaranteed as we see in "You'll Be Back," "Right Hand Man" and "Stay Alive."

"GUNS AND SHIPS"

SCENE 16

SUMMARY

With their new tactics, the colonists finally achieve some success in the war. Burr tells us the secret weapon is "America's favorite fighting Frenchman," Lafayette! He confuses the British on the battlefield but secures funds, weapons, and ships from France.

Lafayette believes the war can be won at Yorktown, but they need Hamilton to command one of the battalions. Hamilton is the only man creative and cunning enough to get the job done, plus, Hamilton is fluent in French (remember, France supplied America with reinforcements, which included soldiers). Washington knows Lafayette is right and sends a letter to summon Hamilton back to the war.

Hamilton kisses Eliza goodbye and answers the call. He enters Washington's office with his head held high.

ANALYZING THE SCENE

STORY EVENT

A Story Event is an active change of a universal human value for one or more characters as a result of conflict (one character's desires clash with another's, or an environmental shift changes the value positively or negatively).

A Working Scene contains at least one Story Event. To determine a scene's Story Event, answer these four Socratic questions:

1. What are the characters literally doing—that is, what are their micro on-the-surface actions?

Lafayette fights the British and travels to France to secure aid. He tells Washington they need Hamilton at the Battle of Yorktown.

2. What is the essential tactic of the characters—that is, what above-the-surface macro behaviors are they employing that are linked to a universal human value?

Lafayette wants Washington to give Hamilton command of a battalion in Yorktown. Washington is aware of this and wants to win the war but also not risk Hamilton's life. Still, Washington knows Lafayette is right. They can't win without Hamilton.

3. What beyond-the-surface universal human values have changed for one or more characters in the scene? Which one of those value changes is most important and should be included in the Story Grid Spreadsheet?

The Revolutionary War turns in the colonists' favor thanks to Lafayette's leadership. However, Lafayette knows the war can't be won without Hamilton. He tells Washington they need Hamilton for the Battle of Yorktown, and Washington agrees. Washington sends for Hamilton. Hamilton answers.

Dismissed to Recruited

4. **The Scene Event Synthesis:** What Story Event sums up the scene's on-the-surface actions, essential above-the-surface worldview behavioral tactics, and beyond-the-surface value change? We will enter that event in the Story Grid Spreadsheet.

As the Revolutionary War turns in America's favor, Lafayette convinces Washington to give Hamilton command over a battalion for the Battle of Yorktown.

HOW THE SCENE ABIDES BY THE FIVE COMMANDMENTS OF STORYTELLING

Inciting Incident: Causal. Lafayette convinces France to give the colonists funds, guns, and ships, which turns the war in the colonies' favor.

Turning Point Progressive Complication: Revelatory. Lafayette insists that Washington needs Hamilton to win the war.

Crisis: Irreconcilable goods choice. Washington can recruit Hamilton and have a better chance at winning the war (despite putting Hamilton's life in danger) or fight without Hamilton and risk losing the war.

Climax: Washington agrees with Lafayette and sends a letter to Hamilton. He tells Hamilton troops are waiting for him on the battlefield.

Resolution: Hamilton accepts Washington's invitation.

NOTES

- Although this scene directly impacts Hamilton's success, he doesn't play a large role until the resolution. Instead, Lafayette is convincing Washington to recall his "right-hand man." This is an important moment in Hamilton's story. He has been sent away, valued but dismissed after the Laurens-Lee duel. There's a clue here that Hamilton misses because he's so excited to be back in action. Even while inactive, he earns the respect of others, including those of higher status. His stock has risen despite the fact that he is not physically present. Miranda is dramatizing the difference between what Hamilton wants and what Hamilton needs. He needs to learn when to wait and when to take bold action.

- Even though Hamilton isn't the man to orchestrate his elevation in here, his friendships early in the story start to pay off in a big way. Hamilton will have his time on the battlefield and play a major role in America's victory because of his friends' unyielding support of him.

- Don't be afraid to allow secondary characters to experience their own internal shifts (as long as they don't overshadow the protagonist). Miranda notes that Lafayette struggles to pronounce "anarchy" in "Aaron Burr, Sir," but by "Guns and Ships" he's rapping rapidly and clearly.[1] This is a subtle change we might not pick up at first, but we feel it! This audible change mirrors Lafayette's rise in status from one of the guys hanging out in the tavern to a linchpin in the colonial army. A novelist can't rely on a talented performer to recreate this effect, but like Miranda, they can adjust the dialogue and roles characters play to demonstrate the change. As readers, we can look for these subtle details that make the experience richer and more satisfying.

- Burr's opening question continues the thread of connecting Hamilton's fate to that of the "ragtag volunteer army." Remember we learned that Hamilton, like the colonies, is "young, scrappy, and hungry."

---

1. McCarter and Miranda, *Hamilton: The Revolution*, 118n2.

"HISTORY HAS ITS EYES ON YOU"

SCENE 17

SUMMARY

Washington gives Hamilton command of a battalion. During this exchange, the general also shares an important lesson he learned from a big mistake early in his career.

As a young officer, Washington led troops into a massacre. He feels the shame and weight of his mistakes but also knows people see and remember what he's done. Washington shares the inevitable truth that, from this moment forward, history will have its eyes on Hamilton, who listens with respect and consideration. He is prepared to fight in the battle but also acknowledges that this and all his actions going forward will impact his legacy.

He is ready.

ANALYZING THE SCENE

STORY EVENT

A Story Event is an active change of a universal human value for one or more characters as a result of conflict (one character's desires clash with another's, or an environmental shift changes the value positively or negatively).

A Working Scene contains at least one Story Event. To determine a scene's Story Event, answer these four Socratic questions:

1. What are the characters literally doing—that is, what are their micro on-the-surface actions?

Hamilton reports for duty, and Washington offers some advice in a private conversation.

2. What is the essential tactic of the characters—that is, what above-the-surface macro behaviors are they employing that are linked to a universal human value?

Washington wants Hamilton to understand he has no control over his legacy and his responsibility is great. Hamilton listens with sincerity and accepts command over his battalion in Yorktown.

3. What beyond-the-surface universal human values have changed for one or more characters in the scene? Which one of those value changes is most important and should be included in the Story Grid Spreadsheet?

Hamilton answers Washington's letter and accepts Washington's request to lead a battalion in the Battle of Yorktown. Washington shares an important lesson he learned as a young boy. Hamilton listens even if he will never fully grasp the lesson's meaning.
  Stalled to Success

4. The Scene Event Synthesis: What Story Event sums up the scene's on-the-surface actions, essential above-the-surface worldview behavioral tactics, and beyond-the-surface value change? We will enter that event in the Story Grid Spreadsheet.

Washington assigns Hamilton a battalion but also warns him that he can't guarantee how people will remember him.

HOW THE SCENE ABIDES BY THE FIVE COMMANDMENTS OF STORYTELLING

Inciting Incident: Causal. Washington summons Hamilton into his office.

Turning Point Progressive Complication: Active. Washington offers Hamilton command over a battalion along with an important lesson that history has its eyes on him.

Crisis: Irreconcilable goods choice. Hamilton can take Washington's lesson to heart or not.

Climax: Hamilton listens respectfully to Washington's lesson, and it appears he takes this seriously, but it's unclear if he will follow through with this wisdom.

Resolution: Hamilton prepares for the Battle of Yorktown a little wiser.

NOTES

- Washington assigns Hamilton his first command and shares one of the most painful and important lessons he's learned in his life. "History has its eyes on" everyone. *Always.* In other words, people can do their best, but history—or the people who narrate history—always have the last word. Washington reflects on how his legacy can be altered by whoever tells his story after his death.
- Washington is known for his major achievements, but what makes him a strong mentor is his willingness to share his mistakes and the hard lessons a life in command has taught him. We don't get the full details in the scene (read Ron Chernow's book *Washington: A Life* if you want to find out

more), but we learn that as a young military commander, Washington "led my men straight into a massacre," and many died because of his mistakes. Washington knows first-hand that people pay attention to what public figures do. No one can control how others will present your story. The burden of the deaths he feels responsible for is a constant weight Washington carries but also a major reminder of the seriousness of his decisions.

- Washington tries to share this important lesson with Hamilton, and while he listens intently to his mentor, we get the sense it's a lesson Hamilton never fully grasps. At moments Hamilton embraces it—like his decision to stick to the plan in Yorktown—but these moments are fleeting after the war. This inability to heed Washington's advice is a major convention setting up the Status Tragic story. Our protagonist longs to rise but also refuses to fully mature and change.

"YORKTOWN (THE WORLD TURNED UPSIDE DOWN)" AND "WHAT COMES NEXT"

SCENE 18

SUMMARY

Before the Battle of Yorktown, Hamilton greets Lafayette, and they discuss their roles in the secret plan before rallying their troops and moving into action. For a brief moment, Hamilton fantasizes about building his legacy by dying as a martyr. But Hamilton reflects momentarily on how Eliza, pregnant with his son, is also counting on him to come home. Hamilton sticks to the plan and commands his troops to move forward with guns unloaded to preserve the advantage of surprise.

Meanwhile Lafayette waits for the British in the Chesapeake Bay, and Hercules Mulligan spies on the British troops. After a week of fighting, the British surrender.

Soldiers, "black and white" alike, contemplate what the victory means for them. Washington answers with the hard truth that freedom will "not yet" be extended to everyone.

Washington negotiates the terms of peace. The British soldiers are escorted out of Yorktown while everyone sings to signify the start of the American nation, "The world turned upside down."

Acting as further resolution of this scene, King George III asks, "What Comes Next?" Governing the new nation will be the real chal-

82

lenge as the American battle commanders take up their new positions as politicians to quarrel and rise or fall.

ANALYZING THE SCENE

STORY EVENT

A Story Event is an active change of a universal human value for one or more characters as a result of conflict (one character's desires clash with another's, or an environmental shift changes the value positively or negatively).

A Working Scene contains at least one Story Event. To determine a scene's Story Event, answer these four Socratic questions:

1. What are the characters literally doing—that is, what are their micro on-the-surface actions?

Hamilton and the other colonial soldiers fight in the Battle of Yorktown.

2. What is the essential tactic of the characters—that is, what above-the-surface macro behaviors are they employing that are linked to a universal human value?

Hamilton and his comrades want to win the Revolutionary War by defeating the British in a decisive battle. They have a plan but need everything to go perfectly for it to work since they are often outnumbered by the British.

3. What beyond-the-surface universal human values have changed for one or more characters in the scene? Which one of those value

changes is most important and should be included in the Story Grid Spreadsheet?

Hamilton greets Lafayette and then leads his troops into battle. Hercules Mulligan has been able to spy on the British government, which aids their victory. The colonists defeat the British, who surrender.

Fighting to Victorious

4. The Scene Event Synthesis: What Story Event sums up the scene's on-the-surface actions, essential above-the-surface worldview behavioral tactics, and beyond-the-surface value change? We will enter that event in the Story Grid Spreadsheet.

Hamilton leads his troops at Yorktown, the final battle in the Revolutionary War. They win and the British surrender.

HOW THE SCENE ABIDES BY THE FIVE COMMANDMENTS OF STORYTELLING

Inciting Incident: Causal. Hamilton takes command of his troops.

Turning Point Progressive Complication: Active. Hamilton remembers Eliza is pregnant and needs him.

Crisis: Best bad choice. Hamilton can fight with the intention of dying as a martyr, or he can heed Washington's lesson as he leads a battalion. He can calmly follow orders.

Climax: Hamilton trusts the plan. He and his troops drive the British to Chesapeake Bay, where Lafayette and his troops are waiting.

Resolution: The British surrender and are escorted out of Yorktown. King George III wonders what will come next. The colonial leaders consider how to build a government.

NOTES

- It's no surprise that Hamilton accepts Washington's call to command. Hamilton expressed a desire to actively fight in a war back in the first scene and has pushed Washington over and over to give him the chance. But we see a change in Hamilton here, probably as the result of Washington's recent advice, but also his time with Eliza. Hamilton is ready to die for his country, and he momentarily fantasizes about building a legacy by dying as a martyr. But he immediately considers the impact on Eliza and his unborn son. Hamilton has people he loves at home, and they are counting on him. He needs to survive. He needs to be smart. He needs to follow Washington's orders for a lot more reasons than his personal dreams of glory. We witness extreme character growth along with his growing success.
- The British surrender is a major turning point for the new nation. Like Hamilton, the colonies gain success. The synchronicity works exceptionally well.
- Remember those external genres mentioned earlier? This scene does a spectacular job at incorporating these external subplots. While I highlighted a status value shift in the analysis, this is also a perfect example of changes in the Society and War values. For Society, we see a change from Suppressed to Powerful. Notice the key word here aligned with a Society genre—power! For War, there's a clear movement toward honorable victory, so you could say something along the lines of a shift from Fighting for Freedom to Honorable Victory.
- The events in "Yorktown" mean freedom for the colonies from Britain. Winning the War for Independence does not secure everyone's freedom, and Washington reminds us of this with his confirmation that freedom is not won "yet" before negotiations begin.
- Lafayette says he will bring freedom to France after this if

they are successful in Yorktown. This sets up a personal element of Hamilton's conflict in "Cabinet Battle #1."

- Miranda notes he changed historical facts in this scene to position Laurens in South Carolina rather than at Yorktown. This allowed him to show Laurens' efforts to secure the rights of three thousand Black men to fight in the war to gain their freedom.[1] This and other adjustments raise an interesting question all historical fiction writers need to ask when drafting their manuscripts. When do you need to alter true events in order to best serve the structure of your story while also upholding the integrity of how history unfolded?
- King George III is a sore loser, but this doesn't take away from the serious question he asks that the new leaders need to consider. "What comes next?" The colonists, while passionate and full of promise, don't know how to govern. They'll need to learn this as they go, and it won't be as easy. It's a huge adjustment.

---

1. McCarter and Miranda, *Hamilton: The Revolution*, 122n5.

"DEAR THEODOSIA" AND "TOMORROW THERE'LL BE MORE OF US"

SCENE 19

SUMMARY

In "Dear Theodosia," Hamilton and Burr sing a lullaby to their newborns (Philip and Theodosia respectively) who were born near the same time. The two ambitious men confess their vulnerabilities and promise to be around for their children. They dream of making a safe and firm foundation for their children where they can grow up to become adults who make a real difference in the world.

In "Tomorrow There'll Be More of Us" Hamilton is distracted from his pledge after receiving news that Laurens has died in service of emancipation. This devastates Hamilton, and he falls silent for a moment thinking of all the work he has to do.

Hamilton tells Eliza he must return to work. "Not throwing away his shot" now includes salvaging Laurens' dream of freedom for all people regardless of color, even at the cost of putting his family second.

ANALYZING THE SCENE

STORY EVENT

A Story Event is an active change of a universal human value for one or more characters as a result of conflict (one character's desires clash with another's, or an environmental shift changes the value positively or negatively).

A Working Scene contains at least one Story Event. To determine a scene's Story Event, answer these four Socratic questions:

1. What are the characters literally doing—that is, what are their micro on-the-surface actions?

Hamilton and Burr sing a lullaby to their newborns. Later, Hamilton reads a letter from Laurens' father.

2. What is the essential tactic of the characters—that is, what above-the-surface macro behaviors are they employing that are linked to a universal human value?

Hamilton and Burr want to make a strong and promising nation for their children's futures, which includes Hamilton's tireless fight for the emancipation of slaves. When news of Laurens' death arrives in a letter from his father, Hamilton forsakes this moment of peace (singing the lullaby and caring for his son, Philip) to continue fighting for his dream.

3. What beyond-the-surface universal human values have changed for one or more characters in the scene? Which one of those value changes is most important and should be included in the Story Grid Spreadsheet?

Hamilton and Burr celebrate the birth of their children, singing a lullaby filled with hope and promise. Laurens' death, however, pulls Hamilton back into the reality of everything he has left to do. He departs in haste.

Peace to Unsettled

4. The Scene Event Synthesis: What Story Event sums up the scene's on-the-surface actions, essential above-the-surface worldview behavioral tactics, and beyond-the-surface value change? We will enter that event in the Story Grid Spreadsheet.

Hamilton and Burr sing a lullaby to their newborns, but Hamilton returns to work after he learns that Laurens has died.

HOW THE SCENE ABIDES BY THE FIVE COMMANDMENTS OF STORYTELLING

Inciting Incident: Causal. Philip and Theodosia are born.

Turning Point Progressive Complication: Revelatory. Hamilton learns of Laurens' death.

Crisis: Irreconcilable goods choice. Hamilton can put his family first—upholding his promise to be around for Philip—or he can actively build the nation he wants for his wife, child, and future children—one that creates freedom and prosperity for all people.

Climax: Hamilton leaves Eliza and Philip to work. This sets the stage for a future where he spends much of his time working and writing.

Resolution: Hamilton takes on his ambitions with a force like never before. He writes feverishly, furiously, and relentlessly for America's future.

NOTES

- Becoming fathers around the same time and the way their hopes and dreams for their children mirror each other are more details that show these men have a lot in common. It's a shame they can't see it and that they could learn a lot from each other.
- Hamilton and Burr sing about how their children will "blow

us all away." We're thinking of this one way in this heartwarming setting, but it's a setup for Philip's heartbreaking scene, "Blow Us All Away."

- Laurens' tragedy is tethered to the sympathy we feel for Hamilton in this scene—something important for a Status Tragic story. We understand why Hamilton is torn between wanting to be with his family and also making the new nation a strong foundation for their well-being. At this moment, he chooses success over his family because he believes it's what's best for them. The tragedy arises from his inability to really understand what is best for his family and what he's willing to sacrifice for success.

"NON-STOP"

SCENE 20

SUMMARY

Hamilton and Burr open separate law practices in New York. Soon Hamilton is recruited for the Constitutional Convention. But people undervalue the importance of the US Constitution. Hamilton seeks Burr's assistance proposing they write and publish anonymous essays to defend the document. Burr declines.

Baffled, Hamilton wonders why Burr doesn't get involved now that they've won the war. Burr is unwilling to take the risk of supporting the losing side. Burr decides to wait while Hamilton engages.

Hamilton recruits James Madison and John Jay to help him write *The Federalist Papers*. Hamilton writes fifty-one of the total eighty-five essays. The US Constitution is soon passed. Washington is asked to serve as president, and he chooses Hamilton to serve as Treasury Secretary. He accepts.

At home, Eliza is torn between her support for Hamilton's goals and her longing to play a larger role in his life.

ANALYZING THE SCENE

STORY EVENT

A Story Event is an active change of a universal human value for one or more characters as a result of conflict (one character's desires clash with another's, or an environmental shift changes the value positively or negatively).

A Working Scene contains at least one Story Event. To determine a scene's Story Event, answer these four Socratic questions:

1. What are the characters literally doing—that is, what are their micro on-the-surface actions?

The founding fathers put ideas into action in order to build a government for the new nation.

2. What is the essential tactic of the characters—that is, what above-the-surface macro behaviors are they employing that are linked to a universal human value?

Hamilton wants to contribute to the founding of the new nation and get the US Constitution ratified. Burr wants to rise in the ranks of the political system but not by Hamilton's methods. Washington wants to guide the country as a wise and resourceful leader. Eliza wants Hamilton to get what he wants but also to be a part of his life. She wants him to spend more time with his family. Angelica wants Hamilton to remember her across the sea.

3. What beyond-the-surface universal human values have changed for one or more characters in the scene? Which one of those value changes is most important and should be included in the Story Grid Spreadsheet?

Hamilton opens a law practice and initiates the writing and publication of *The Federalist Papers*. The essays are well-regarded and influence ratification of the US Constitution. Washington is asked to serve as president, and Washington asks Hamilton to join his staff as Treasury Secretary. Hamilton accepts, and although he loves Eliza and Philip, he focuses on the birth of the new nation.

Striving to Success

4. The Scene Event Synthesis: What Story Event sums up the scene's on-the-surface actions, essential above-the-surface worldview behavioral tactics, and beyond-the-surface value change? We will enter that event in the Story Grid Spreadsheet.

To build the new nation, Hamilton writes many of The Federalist Papers, *which assist with the passing of the Constitution of the United States of America.*

HOW THE SCENE ABIDES BY THE FIVE COMMANDMENTS OF STORYTELLING

Inciting Incident: Causal. Hamilton leads the formation of the new legal system as a lawyer and is asked to speak at the Constitutional Convention.

Turning Point Progressive Complication: Active. Burr rejects Hamilton's request to write *The Federalist Papers* in support of the US Constitution.

Crisis: Irreconcilable goods choice. Hamilton can recruit different men to help him write *The Federalist Papers* and anonymously publish them with no guarantee they will help pass the US Constitution, or Hamilton can focus on law and wait (like Burr).

Climax: Hamilton publishes *The Federalist Papers*.

Resolution: The US Constitution is ratified, and Washington is asked to serve as president. Washington asks Hamilton to serve the country with him, working as Treasury Secretary. Hamilton takes his shot. He follows Washington into governmental power, fully aware that Eliza is helpless, and that history has its eyes on him.

NOTES

- Burr's rejection of Hamilton's request to help him write *The Federalist Papers* is one of Burr's major mistakes. He throws away his opportunity to be part of something important and to partner with Hamilton, a rising star, because he's afraid to take a risk. Arguably, Burr's reticence has worked for him so far. He survived the war, but he doesn't see when it makes sense to change his strategy and take a chance on taking a stand.

- This scene illustrates how Hamilton will do anything he needs in order to get what he wants. Multiple voices urge Hamilton toward different paths, some with warnings and others with hard truths. Hamilton overlooks any doubts about his inability to succeed and follows Washington. The last words we hear before the curtains close are Hamilton's declaration that he is not throwing away his shot. Whatever we know or don't about whether Hamilton will throw away his shot, we're enthralled with this marvelously flawed and sympathetic character. We can't wait to see what comes next.

"WHAT'D I MISS?"

SCENE 21

SUMMARY

Burr opens this scene by foreshadowing the conflict that will arise between Hamilton and Jefferson.

Jefferson returns from France where he missed the war while serving as US ambassador. He is summoned to New York right away to serve as Washington's Secretary of State. Madison complains about Hamilton's financial plans and how they amount to "government control." He begs Jefferson to step in and challenge Hamilton.

Jefferson agrees to help before attending his first cabinet meeting.

ANALYZING THE SCENE

STORY EVENT

A Story Event is an active change of a universal human value for one or more characters as a result of conflict (one character's desires clash with another's, or an environmental shift changes the value positively or negatively).

A Working Scene contains at least one Story Event. To determine a scene's Story Event, answer these four Socratic questions:

1. What are the characters literally doing—that is, what are their micro on-the-surface actions?

Jefferson returns to Virginia to find he's been appointed Secretary of State and then travels to NYC where he meets with Madison.

2. What is the essential tactic of the characters—that is, what above-the-surface macro behaviors are they employing that are linked to a universal human value?

Jefferson wants to stop Hamilton's financial plan. He agrees to help Madison prevent Hamilton's financial debt plan from passing, but Hamilton isn't an easy man to stop.

3. What beyond-the-surface universal human values have changed for one or more characters in the scene? Which one of those value changes is most important and should be included in the Story Grid Spreadsheet?

Thomas returns from France, where he was serving as ambassador. He rushes to New York to serve as Secretary of State. Madison warns Jefferson of Hamilton's financial plan and pleads with his friend to fight it. Jefferson accepts the challenge. Hamilton has successfully moved his agenda forward but will now face a formidable opponent.
Complacent to Disturbed

4. The Scene Event Synthesis: What Story Event sums up the scene's on-the-surface actions, essential above-the-surface worldview behavioral tactics, and beyond-the-surface value change? We will enter that event in the Story Grid Spreadsheet.

Thomas Jefferson returns from France and becomes Secretary of State. He promises to challenge Hamilton's financial debt plan.

HOW THE SCENE ABIDES BY THE FIVE COMMANDMENTS OF STORYTELLING

Inciting Incident: Causal. Thomas Jefferson returns home (Virginia).

Turning Point Progressive Complication: Revelatory. Madison updates Jefferson on Hamilton's financial plan and asks for Jefferson's help.

Crisis: Best bad choice. Jefferson can ignore Hamilton's financial plan and allow it to become "government control" or he can challenge Hamilton, most likely creating an enemy and potentially jeopardizing Washington's support.

Climax: Jefferson prepares for his first cabinet meeting with Madison to address the financial debt plan. He intends to speak out against Hamilton.

Resolution: Jefferson attends the cabinet meeting.

NOTES

- Burr once again sets the scene for the audience, checking in on where Hamilton is (serving as Secretary of the Treasury) and introducing a new player on the scene, Jefferson. Burr foreshadows the conflict that will arise between the two men. Jefferson's immediate goal is to help their mutual friend Lafayette achieve freedom from the monarchy in France.
- This scene sets up later events by establishing Jefferson's character. The reference to Sally Hemmings in the lyrics is a subtle reminder that Jefferson has had an affair with one of

his female slaves. This fact doesn't prevent him from using Hamilton's affair against him to achieve his political goals.

- **Fun Fact:** In the second half of the story, you'll probably notice that the same actors who play Hamilton's friends in the first half of the story become antagonists later. Even though each character flips allegiance, the lines in the opening scene, "Alexander Hamilton" apply to both roles. The meaning of "We fought with him" depends on your perspective. Similarly the actor who plays Laurens (Anthony Ramos) returns as Hamilton's son, Philip, and he is someone who "dies for him."[1] That's clever, but how does this help us as writers? The key takeaways here are that tight constraints can often be a recipe for innovation and paying close attention to a master storyteller's decisions can reveal those micro acts of genius.

---

1. McCarter and Miranda, *Hamilton: The Revolution*, 17n9.

"CABINET BATTLE #1"
SCENE 22

SUMMARY

In this scene, Jefferson challenges Hamilton's plan for the financial system. Jefferson doesn't propose an alternative to the plan but questions why states without debt, like Virginia, should pay off other states' debts. He warns that Hamilton's plan is similar to the way British raised revenue from the colonies by taxing goods.

Hamilton suggests that Jefferson is naïve about what it takes to govern and uninformed since he's been away for so long. Contrary to Jefferson's claims, the debt restructuring will allow the nation to seek credit. Hamilton notes Virginia carries no debt because slaveholders exploit Black Americans and that opponents of the plan have no better alternative. He finishes his address by insulting Jefferson.

Washington interrupts the debate and orders Hamilton to seek more votes from Congress. If Hamilton doesn't convince the cabinet to pass his plan, he will lose his position.

ANALYZING THE SCENE

STORY EVENT

A Story Event is an active change of a universal human value for one or more characters as a result of conflict (one character's desires clash with another's, or an environmental shift changes the value positively or negatively).

A Working Scene contains at least one Story Event. To determine a scene's Story Event, answer these four Socratic questions:

1. What are the characters literally doing—that is, what are their micro on-the-surface actions?

Hamilton and Jefferson debate the financial plan. Washington takes Hamilton aside to tell him he needs to find a compromise.

2. What is the essential tactic of the characters—that is, what above-the-surface macro behaviors are they employing that are linked to a universal human value?

Hamilton wants Congress to pass his financial plan. Jefferson, Hamilton's rising political opponent, wants to defeat Hamilton's financial plan by convincing Congress to reject it. Washington wants Hamilton to realize they aren't at war and governing requires compromise.

3. What beyond-the-surface universal human values have changed for one or more characters in the scene? Which one of those value changes is most important and should be included in the Story Grid Spreadsheet?

Hamilton and Jefferson present their positions on the financial plan, and while Jefferson focuses on playing the crowd-pleaser, Hamilton challenges Jefferson's points with logic and fact. Hamilton's rudeness causes Washington to interrupt the debate. Hamilton argues with Washington in private but ultimately accepts that he needs to win more votes to get Congressional approval for his plan even though it's not something Hamilton wants to spend time managing.

Success to Failure

4. The Scene Event Synthesis: What Story Event sums up the scene's on-the-surface actions, essential above-the-surface worldview behavioral tactics, and beyond-the-surface value change? We will enter that event in the Story Grid Spreadsheet.

Hamilton and Jefferson debate Hamilton's financial debt plan, and Hamilton fails to get the votes needed to pass it.

HOW THE SCENE ABIDES BY THE FIVE COMMANDMENTS OF STORYTELLING

Inciting Incident: Causal. Washington calls a cabinet meeting to discuss Hamilton's financial plan.

Turning Point Progressive Complication: Active. Washington calls a recess after Hamilton has an inappropriate outburst.

Crisis: Best bad choice. Hamilton can figure out a more sophisticated way to get votes (like a compromise) or not.

Climax: Hamilton suffers disappointment as Jefferson and Madison chant that he doesn't have the votes. In private, Washington warns Hamilton that he needs to find a better way to get votes from Congress (find a compromise) or risk a call for his removal, and Hamilton argues against this direction—but also knows Washington is right.

Resolution: Though annoyed, Hamilton knows Washington is right. Hamilton leaves the debate a failure and in need of a new plan to get votes.

- One major complication that disrupts Hamilton's poise in this scene is when Jefferson accuses Hamilton of serving his own interests with the financial plan, to which Hamilton emphatically answers, "Not true!" Jefferson's false accusation directly challenges Hamilton's motivations and his commitment to his values, which adds fuel to his zealous response. Remember Hamilton is obsessed with his legacy, but he doesn't ever intentionally risk harm to the new nation. While absolutely problematic, Jefferson's accusation doesn't quite thrust Hamilton into his Crisis. Another way to say this is that it doesn't begin to shift the value in the scene and is not the Turning Point Progressive Complication. But when Washington calls a recess and states clearly that Hamilton doesn't have the votes, his financial plan is in serious jeopardy.
- When Hamilton says, "Not True!" in response to Jefferson's accusation of bad faith, the tenor of the debate changes. Had Hamilton not taken it personally, he could have issued a cold, logical recitation of the financial facts of the financial plan. But he gets emotional and talks too much, which causes Washington to call for the break. This demonstrates one of Hamilton's flaws and a need for a worldview shift.
- Jefferson's way of operating presents a major threat to Hamilton because the Virginian can goad him into outbursts. Jefferson is a crowd-pleaser, sophisticated like Burr, but willing to act like Hamilton. He is self-possessed and not quick to anger. Jefferson employs the positive tactics of both men. Is it any wonder he survives while Burr and Hamilton destroy one another?
- Hamilton could learn from Jefferson, and he seems to adopt some of his negotiation skills to gain Jefferson's support for the financial system in "The Room Where It Happens." Hamilton often fails to "read the room," though. His bold

moves helped him achieve success in the past, especially when convincing colonists to join the fight or literally fighting in battle. But it rarely works when it comes to political negotiation.

"TAKE A BREAK"

SCENE 23

SUMMARY

Hamilton writes to Angelica to seek advice to get his financial plan through Congress.

Eliza interrupts to have him come see what nine-year-old Philip has accomplished. Philip raps a poem for his father, and Hamilton is impressed. For a moment he promises to try to join his family upstate that summer.

Later, Angelica's response arrives. She wants Hamilton to keep fighting for his financial plan but also to join Eliza and their family upstate because Angelica will be there too. She wonders if he intentionally changed the comma in his letter to create a more tender address, "My dearest, Angelica."

Angelica arrives in New York to a joyful reunion with Eliza. Unfortunately, Hamilton has decided he cannot join them because he will lose his job if he doesn't get Congress to pass his plan. He stays behind while Eliza and Angelica travel upstate with the family.

ANALYZING THE SCENE

STORY EVENT

A Story Event is an active change of a universal human value for one or more characters as a result of conflict (one character's desires clash with another's, or an environmental shift changes the value positively or negatively).

A Working Scene contains at least one Story Event. To determine a scene's Story Event, answer these four Socratic questions:

1. What are the characters literally doing—that is, what are their micro on-the-surface actions?

Hamilton exchanges letters with Angelica and has conversations with Eliza as they work out plans for the summer.

2. What is the essential tactic of the characters—that is, what above-the-surface macro behaviors are they employing that are linked to a universal human value?

Hamilton wants Congress to pass his financial debt plan. He also wants Angelica's political advice. Angelica wants Hamilton emotionally, but she also wants good things and happiness for her sister Eliza. They exchange letters that insinuate an emotional affair since they never have a physical one. Eliza wants Hamilton to take a break and spend some time with the family, but his determination to pass his financial debt plan continually prevents this.

3. What beyond-the-surface universal human values have changed for one or more characters in the scene? Which one of those value changes is most important and should be included in the Story Grid Spreadsheet?

Hamilton writes to Angelica with urgency, frustration, and vulnerability about his inability to get the votes he needs to pass his plan. He seeks Angelica's advice on what to do and initially shrugs off Eliza's invitation to come downstairs. Eventually, he joins Eliza and is impressed and entertained by his son Philip. He considers taking Eliza up on her invitation to take a break but redirects his attention after receiving Angelica's response. Even when Angelica arrives in the states to join Eliza and their family upstate, Hamilton stays behind to work.

Distracted to Focused

4. The Scene Event Synthesis: What Story Event sums up the scene's on-the-surface actions, essential above-the-surface worldview behavioral tactics, and beyond-the-surface value change? We will enter that event in the Story Grid Spreadsheet.

Hamilton seeks Angelica's advice on how to get votes for his financial debt plan while Eliza tries to get Hamilton to spend time with the family, but he keeps working.

HOW THE SCENE ABIDES BY THE FIVE COMMANDMENTS OF STORYTELLING

Inciting Incident: Causal. Eliza asks Hamilton to take a break.

Turning Point Progressive Complication: Revelatory. Angelica's letter arrives encouraging Hamilton to "get through to Jefferson" but also to join her and his family upstate.

Crisis: Best bad choice. Hamilton can join Eliza, Angelica, and his family at risk of losing votes for his financial plan, or he can reject Eliza and Angelica's invitation, despite his and their disappointment, to stay home and work.

Climax: Hamilton rejects the invitation to join the family.

Resolution: The family travels upstate without Hamilton.

NOTES

- Hamilton and Angelica are obviously attracted to one another, but unlike the physical affair Hamilton has in the next scene, Hamilton's affair with Angelica is emotional, carried on through flirtatious letters.
- Notice how Hamilton seeks Angelica's advice in his opening letter. This is a testament to Hamilton's sincere respect for her. She is one of the few characters he values for their intelligence.
- Character dynamics and relationships are important to master as a writer, and Miranda illustrates the affection and trust Angelica and Hamilton share in her subtle, witty attempt at persuading Hamilton to join her, which plays out with an allusion quoting Shakespeare. Miranda references several musical and literary works in his lyrics, but the reference to *Macbeth* in this scene suggests a shared language or ritual between Hamilton and Angelica.
- If you're a big Story Grid fan, you may recall Story Grid creator, Shawn Coyne, identifying the intellectual banter between Elizabeth Bennett and Fitzwilliam Darcy as a sign that they are made for each other in *Pride and Prejudice by Jane Austen: A Story Grid Masterwork Analysis Guide*. Shared rituals are a convention of the Love Story.
- What's interesting is how Angelica inspires and mentors Hamilton in a way he respects and enjoys, but Eliza grounds and supports him in a way he needs, even if it takes Hamilton some time to fully grasp this.

"SAY NO TO THIS"
SCENE 24

SUMMARY

Hamilton confesses to feeling exhausted and lonely when he first encounters Maria Reynolds. She asks Hamilton for help from her abusive husband, and Hamilton, out of pity, gives her the money in his pocket and walks her home. She asks Hamilton to stay, and despite Hamilton's wish to decline, he and Maria begin their affair.

After multiple encounters, Hamilton receives a letter from Maria's husband, James Reynolds, warning him that if Hamilton doesn't pay, Eliza will learn of the affair. Reynolds will allow Hamilton to keep seeing Maria if Hamilton continues to pay.

Hamilton decides to pay Reynolds and continue his affair with Maria.

ANALYZING THE SCENE

STORY EVENT

A Story Event is an active change of a universal human value for one or more characters as a result of conflict (one character's desires clash with another's, or an environmental shift changes the value positively or negatively).

A Working Scene contains at least one Story Event. To determine a scene's Story Event, answer these four Socratic questions:

1. **What are the characters literally doing—that is, what are their micro on-the-surface actions?**

Hamilton and Maria Reynolds have an affair while Hamilton is working and his family is away.

2. **What is the essential tactic of the characters—that is, what above-the-surface macro behaviors are they employing that are linked to a universal human value?**

Hamilton wants an affair with Maria. Maria, likewise, wants Hamilton. James Reynolds wants to blackmail Hamilton.

3. **What beyond-the-surface universal human values have changed for one or more characters in the scene? Which one of those value changes is most important and should be included in the Story Grid Spreadsheet?**

Hamilton becomes exhausted and lonely while working on his financial plan when Maria appears at his front door. Feeling pity and attraction for Maria, Hamilton engages in an affair. Later, Maria's husband, James Reynolds, blackmails Hamilton. To keep him quiet, Hamilton pays him off, despite knowing what he is doing is wrong.
Honorable to Deceitful

4. **The Scene Event Synthesis: What Story Event sums up the scene's on-the-surface actions, essential above-the-surface worldview behavioral tactics, and beyond-the-surface value change? We will enter that event in the Story Grid Spreadsheet.**

Exhausted and weak, Hamilton engages in an affair with Maria Reynolds while trying to get his financial debt plan passed.

HOW THE SCENE ABIDES BY THE FIVE COMMANDMENTS OF STORYTELLING

Inciting Incident: Causal. Maria asks Hamilton for help.

Turning Point Progressive Complication: Active. Reynolds blackmails Hamilton.

Crisis: Best bad choice. Hamilton can confess his infidelity to Eliza and risk ruining his reputation and marriage, or Hamilton can pay Reynolds (and continue the affair) while depending on him to keep quiet.

Climax: Hamilton pays off Reynolds and continues the affair.

Resolution: Hamilton hopes nobody finds out about his affair and continues to put money aside to pay off Reynolds so he can continue his relationship with Maria.

NOTES

- Even as Hamilton accuses Maria of purposefully playing a role in this con, he declares out loud, "How could I do this?" acknowledging that he's to blame for the mistakes and harm he causes both his reputation and marriage.[1] This awareness shakes his confidence. Knowingly succumbing to temptation marks the first major mistake of several for Hamilton. He can argue that his bold actions and relentless work serve him and his family by creating a firm foundation for the nation. But his affair is a selfish act that serves no one, and here he shows that he knows it.
- In a cautionary Status Tragic story, the protagonist makes

mistakes that ruin their chances for success. Hamilton's affair with Maria Reynolds marks the beginning of the end of Hamilton's political career—but not because he has the affair. Although he says, "I'm ruined," that's not guaranteed at this point. His fatal fall occurs *because* of this affair, but the affair itself does not sabotage Hamilton's public and private life.

- Desperate to protect herself from if not escape her abusive husband, Maria plays the role of a damsel in distress. While her body language suggests her sexual intentions, we're left to wonder if she was part of the con. Did she knowingly participate in her husband's plan to bribe Hamilton? Did she really fall for Hamilton? Or both? Sometimes not knowing the answers to big questions troubling the protagonist can escalate the tension and internal conflict.

- Even though Hamilton thinks he can cover up his mistakes by paying off James Reynolds, he can't take back what he's done. Still, the truth that could ruin his reputation and marriage will always remain a lingering threat. Writers should consider how reversible the protagonist's decisions are. Hamilton can't undo this betrayal. He has options in how he deals with it, but he can no longer go back to the way things were. The closer to the end of the story we get, the more character decisions should become irreversible. For example, Hamilton crosses another line when he tells Jefferson, Madison, and Burr about the affair.

- Two important moments in this scene could arguably work as the Turning Point: Hamilton's decision to act on the affair with Maria, and the arrival of Reynolds' letter demanding money to keep quiet. Ultimately, what determines a Turning Point Progressive Complication is how it forces a character into a Crisis and how it begins to shift the value at stake in the scene. Hamilton moves from Honorable to Deceitful when he fails to take responsibility for his actions and continues the affair.

- The affair threatens the global value, *Success*, both in the short and long term. Hamilton moves toward *Selling Out*. This is what we call the negation of the negation on the value gradient. He's acted to repair damage but not in a way that honors his family or his moral code. The value shift specific to this scene is described with different words, *Honorable to Deceitful*, but we can see how this shift affects his success. Hamilton is moving away from Success and toward *Selling Out* because the pressure and ability to succeed is siphoned away by Hamilton's deception of Eliza.
- The unexpected event that puts Hamilton's success most at stake in this scene is when he reads Reynolds' letter. It forces Hamilton into a Crisis where he must decide whether to sacrifice and do the right thing or continue to betray Eliza and cover it up by spending his own funds. In other words, he's taking from his family in another way.
- Hamilton's choice to pursue the affair with Maria moves him from fidelity to infidelity, but this feels less important than Hamilton's recognition of what he's done, which Reynolds' letter brings to his attention. Without Reynolds, Hamilton might have gotten away with his affair and avoided the self-sabotage he undertakes later in the story. Bottom line, when analyzing your own scenes, spend less time looking for the perfect words to define your life value shift and focus on how the Turning Point Progressive Complication initiates a value shift and forces a Crisis that causes movement along the global value gradient.
- Miranda substitutes "Fuuuu—" for the curse word, and everyone knows exactly what this means. Writers can use this brilliant technique to add humor in a particularly tense moment for a release. Resorting to swear words can feel cheap to a reader or audience depending on the context. Miranda's strategy to suggest but not use the curse successfully elicits the desired reaction from the audience— a laugh in the midst of an extremely serious threat. The

word is used elsewhere for different reasons, but its absence can be as powerful as its presence.

———————————————————

1. McCarter and Miranda, *Hamilton: The Revolution*, 178n4.

"THE ROOM WHERE IT HAPPENS" AND "SCHUYLER DEFEATED"

SCENE 25

SUMMARY

Hamilton encounters Burr, who asks his friend how he's planning to get his financial plan passed. Hamilton says he'll try Burr's strategy, "Talk less. Smile more." Madison calls Hamilton away, and Burr is aware he's being left out of the negotiations.

Only Jefferson's account of this meeting remains, so we hear of the events from his perspective. The result is a compromise. Jefferson and Madison will support the financial plan, and Hamilton will support moving the capital to Virginia.

Burr realizes he can't wait any longer. He switches political parties to run against and defeat Hamilton's father-in-law, Philip Schuyler, to become the senator from New York. Hamilton feels betrayed.

ANALYZING THE SCENE

STORY EVENT

A Story Event is an active change of a universal human value for one or more characters as a result of conflict (one character's desires clash with another's, or an environmental shift changes the value positively or negatively).

A Working Scene contains at least one Story Event. To determine a scene's Story Event, answer these four Socratic questions:

1. What are the characters literally doing—that is, what are their micro on-the-surface actions?

Hamilton speaks with Burr and then negotiates with Jefferson and Madison. Burr observes events from afar and then runs against and defeats Philip Schuyler to become a senator from New York.

2. What is the essential tactic of the characters—that is, what above-the-surface macro behaviors are they employing that are linked to a universal human value?

Hamilton wants to get his financial debt plan passed. Burr wants to be involved in the decision-making process of governing the new nation. Jefferson and Madison want the capital relocated to Virginia.

3. What beyond-the-surface universal human values have changed for one or more characters in the scene? Which one of those value changes is most important and should be included in the Story Grid Spreadsheet?

Hamilton accepts Jefferson's dinner invitation. Over dinner, they negotiate terms that end with support for Hamilton's financial plan if Hamilton backs Virginia for the nation's capital. Longing for a place in the government, Burr can't believe Hamilton accomplishes his goals. Burr switches parties to run for Senate. He starts to act in order to get what he wants. Burr successfully runs against Schuyler for Senate.

Failure to Compromise to Success

4. The Scene Event Synthesis: What Story Event sums up the scene's

on-the-surface actions, essential above-the-surface worldview behavioral tactics, and beyond-the-surface value change? We will enter that event in the Story Grid Spreadsheet.

Hamilton successfully negotiates to secure his financial plan. Burr runs for Senate against Schuyler.

HOW THE SCENE ABIDES BY THE FIVE COMMANDMENTS OF STORYTELLING

Inciting Incident: Causal. Jefferson and Madison invite Hamilton to dinner in order to negotiate a compromise.

Turning Point Progressive Complication: Revelatory. Madison and Jefferson propose a quid pro quo. They will back Hamilton's financial debt plan if Hamilton supports relocating the capital to Virginia.

Crisis: Irreconcilable goods choice. Hamilton can compromise his ideals in order to partake in the quid pro quo, or he can look for another way to gain their support (and probably fail).

Climax: Hamilton supports the capital's move to Virginia and gains Jefferson and Madison's support; he gets his debt plan passed and gloats about this to Burr.

Resolution: Hamilton gains some headway as a founding father; however, he's agitated Burr. Hamilton's father-in-law loses to Burr in the race for senator as a result.

NOTES

- We are told no one really knows what happened during the dinner since the only historical documents retelling the events are from Jefferson's perspective. Jefferson claims Hamilton was desperate to find support for his financial debt plan, so Jefferson arranged a dinner meeting with

Hamilton, Madison, and him to discuss it. Hamilton convinces them to back his financial plan in exchange for moving the nation's capital to Virginia.

- Burr wants to be included, but Hamilton bluntly explains you have to take risks if you want to participate in decision-making. Burr never wins because he waits on the sidelines to see who will come out on top. Hamilton admits that taking decisive action wins him supporters and haters, but ultimately, he makes things happen.

- In this scene, Hamilton and Burr joke about legacy before Hamilton walks into a meeting where decisions are made that have lasted through today. They talk about how General Mercer's legacy is secure (he will be remembered) because he died as a martyr in the Revolutionary War and now a street is named after him. Hamilton and Burr joke about this, but then Madison calls Hamilton to dinner. To make things worse, Hamilton says he intends to get his debt plan supported by following Burr's advice. "Talk less. Smile more."

- Both Hamilton and Burr have important value shifts in this scene, and each has a Turning Point that forces them into a Crisis. Ultimately, Hamilton's shift is more important since he is the protagonist of the story, but this scene is a perfect example of why antagonists are so important, and why you should develop these characters as much as your protagonist. The escalating conflict raises the stakes from beginning to end. And don't forget, the antagonist is the protagonist of his or her own story.

- From Burr's perspective, the Five Commandments go this way. Hamilton and Burr discuss legacy (causal Inciting Incident). Hamilton gets his debt plan passed by taking a page from Burr's playbook, talking less, smiling more (revelatory Turning Point Progressive Complication). Burr can continue talking less and smiling more, or he can take charge of his own successes, despite how this impacts his friendship with Hamilton (best bad choice Crisis). Burr switches political parties to run against Philip Schuyler for his Senate seat and wins (Climax). Burr gains political success but damages his friendship with Alexander Hamilton (Resolution).

- It's not until this scene that we actually understand what Burr *wants*. He finally answers Hamilton's question, "What do you want, Burr?" Miranda notes he wants to be in the room "for the sake of it."[1]

- Knowing that Burr wants to be in the room Hamilton constantly has access to—in other words, Hamilton is able to influence decisions on the nation's beginnings and Burr is not—escalates the stakes in instrumental ways. We see Burr's bitterness of Hamilton start to influence his actions. Not coincidentally, this marks the first time Hamilton acknowledges that in order to get his plan passed he needs to act more like Burr. Burr finds this gratifying until Hamilton actually gets what he wants by behaving exactly how Burr has all along.

- The rivalry between Hamilton and Jefferson and Madison endures despite the compromise, but Burr rises up as an increasingly dangerous threat to Hamilton's status because he was left out. In this light, notice how Hamilton's actions in this scene (moving him toward success) serve not only as a Turning Point for Hamilton's success, but also Burr's. As the scene moves into "Schuyler Defeated," we see how Hamilton and Burr move in tandem toward success, though in wildly different ways. Hamilton gains success in "The Room Where It Happens" by negotiating, and Burr finally accepts what he needs to do in order to gain such success and define his legacy. This pays off in "Schuyler Defeated." Their fates are braided together. Their actions in these scenes portray genius setups that inevitably pay off in unforgettable ways as they come the final showdown— when Hamilton accepts Burr's duel.

- **Fun Facts from history:** Although nobody really knows what was said during Hamilton's dinner with Jefferson and

Madison, a meeting was held on June 20, 1790 that Jefferson hosted and Hamilton and Madison attended. Out of it came the "Compromise of 1790."[2]

---

1. McCarter and Miranda, *Hamilton: The Revolution*, 189n7.
2. "The Compromise of 1790," National Archives, accessed January 16, 2021, https://prologue.blogs.archives.gov/2015/05/31/the-compromise-of-1790/.

"CABINET BATTLE #2"

SCENE 26

SUMMARY

Washington listens to Jefferson and Hamilton debate whether America should send troops to aid the French in their war against Britain.

Jefferson argues they have a duty to support their allies. America signed a treaty because France sent aid to support the colonists in the Revolutionary War. Hamilton argues aiding the French will end in disaster because the country is in chaos without a leader. The agreement was made with the king, and he's been executed. Washington agrees with Hamilton and asks him to draft a statement of neutrality.

Jefferson criticizes Hamilton for being disloyal to his friend Lafayette and suggests that Hamilton's political success is due to Washington's favor. As the president calls for Hamilton from off stage, Jefferson taunts, "Daddy's calling."

ANALYZING THE SCENE

STORY EVENT

A Story Event is an active change of a universal human value for one or more characters as a result of conflict (one character's desires clash with another's, or an environmental shift changes the value positively or negatively).

A Working Scene contains at least one Story Event. To determine a scene's Story Event, answer these four Socratic questions:

1. What are the characters literally doing—that is, what are their micro on-the-surface actions?

Hamilton and Jefferson debate whether America should support the French in their war against Britain.

2. What is the essential tactic of the characters—that is, what above-the-surface macro behaviors are they employing that are linked to a universal human value?

Hamilton wants Washington to remain neutral. Jefferson wants Washington to support their French allies. Washington wants to make the best decision for his people and country.

3. What beyond-the-surface universal human values have changed for one or more characters in the scene? Which one of those value changes is most important and should be included in the Story Grid Spreadsheet?

Uncertain of what to do, Washington calls a cabinet meeting where Hamilton and Jefferson debate supporting the French. Each makes their case, and Washington—likely already leaning toward neutrality—sides with Hamilton. Confident in his decision to draft a statement of neutrality, Washington leaves Jefferson and Hamilton behind, where they exchange bitter remarks with one another.

Dominating to Success

4. The Scene Event Synthesis: What Story Event sums up the scene's on-the-surface actions, essential above-the-surface worldview behavioral tactics, and beyond-the-surface value change? We will enter that event in the Story Grid Spreadsheet.

Jefferson and Hamilton debate America's potential support of the French, and Washington determines the nation should remain neutral.

HOW THE SCENE ABIDES BY THE FIVE COMMANDMENTS OF STORYTELLING

Inciting Incident: Causal. Washington calls a cabinet meeting.

Turning Point Progressive Complication: Revelatory. Hamilton explains that the people are rioting and have no leader.

Crisis: Irreconcilable goods choice. Washington can side with Jefferson and hold true to the treaty but risk America's fragile state, or he can side with Hamilton and draft a statement of neutrality.

Climax: Washington asks Hamilton to draft a statement of neutrality and defends his decision to Jefferson.

Resolution: Jefferson badgers Hamilton, suggesting the only reason for his success is that he has Washington in "his pocket." Washington summons Hamilton, who appears to wonder if Jefferson is right.

NOTES

- An interesting factor driving this scene is the tension between Jefferson and Hamilton after Washington decides to pause the meeting in the Climax. This makes the Resolution of the scene feel almost like a scene itself since it focuses on Hamilton's internal debate (and fear), which Jefferson calls out. Washington favors Hamilton, and this is why Hamilton is successful. This is one of the few times in the story Hamilton doesn't have a comeback. Instead, he exits in response to Washington's call, leaving the audience to feel the bitterness long after the scene ends. It also reinforces Hamilton's vulnerabilities immediately after he achieves a big victory in the cabinet, which again humanizes him and his obsession with status/station and legacy.

- The war between France and Britain is a great subject for a debate in "Cabinet Battle #2." However, only Washington can make the final decision on what to do about getting involved in foreign conflicts. Washington is in the best position to face the scene's Crisis.

- Washington does favor Hamilton. Do you think this is the only reason Hamilton thrives, like Jefferson suggests, or do you think Hamilton would have risen regardless? Do you think this internal recognition on Hamilton's part further emphasizes his desperation to secure his legacy? Notice how Hamilton's greatest fears also unmask his greatest wants. In this way, we focus on where he's most terrified of failing. At this moment, he's completely blind to what he needs.

- Hamilton can relish winning the debate, but he feeds Jefferson's belief that his successes are a result of Washington's favoritism. If he chooses to argue, he jeopardizes future support from Washington. This silences Hamilton, which rarely happens.

"WASHINGTON ON YOUR SIDE"

SCENE 27

SUMMARY

Frustrated with Hamilton's success and the effects of the financial plan on farmers and veterans, Jefferson tells Burr he wants to find a way to neutralize his rival. Madison arrives and suggests they investigate Treasury Department spending, and unless they act, they are complicit.

Jefferson realizes he can't challenge Hamilton from inside the cabinet because Washington won't listen. He decides to resign his position as Secretary of State.

ANALYZING THE SCENE

STORY EVENT

A Story Event is an active change of a universal human value for one or more characters as a result of conflict (one character's desires clash with another's, or an environmental shift changes the value positively or negatively).

A Working Scene contains at least one Story Event. To determine a scene's Story Event, answer these four Socratic questions:

1. What are the characters literally doing—that is, what are their micro on-the-surface actions?

Jefferson, Madison, and Burr scheme against Hamilton.

2. What is the essential tactic of the characters—that is, what above-the-surface macro behaviors are they employing that are linked to a universal human value?

Jefferson, Madison, and Burr want to stop Hamilton's financial debt plan from jeopardizing the lives of the poor (like veterans) for the benefit of the rich's well-being and control—in addition to sabotaging his career because they are jealous of his success. They envy Washington's support of Hamilton and believe they can ruin him by tracking the money in the Treasury (in hopes of finding evidence of Hamilton's corrupt motives).

3. What beyond-the-surface universal human values have changed for one or more characters in the scene? Which one of those value changes is most important and should be included in the Story Grid Spreadsheet?

Jefferson, Madison, and Burr feel disadvantaged and unheard, but after they craft a plan to take Hamilton out, they feel empowered by their scheme.
Marginalized to Empowered

4. The Scene Event Synthesis: What Story Event sums up the scene's on-the-surface actions, essential above-the-surface worldview behavioral tactics, and beyond-the-surface value change? We will enter that event in the Story Grid Spreadsheet.

Burr, Jefferson, and Madison discuss ways to bring down Hamilton and decide to investigate the Treasury.

HOW THE SCENE ABIDES BY THE FIVE COMMANDMENTS OF STORYTELLING

Inciting Incident: Causal. Hamilton wins the cabinet discussion about France, and Washington asks him to draft a statement of neutrality.

Turning Point Progressive Complication: Revelatory. Madison suggests that they try to find something to ruin Hamilton's reputation.

Crisis: Irreconcilable goods choice. They can investigate where the money goes within the Treasury and hopefully find information they can use against Hamilton, or they can remain passive and allow the centralizing of national credit to hinder the poor while benefiting the rich.

Climax: Jefferson, Madison, and Burr agree to investigate. Jefferson proclaims he needs to resign in order to challenge Washington and Hamilton.

Resolution: The three men actively seek information on Hamilton's personal gain from the Treasury.

NOTES

- Miranda notes that Jefferson is right about the negative consequences of the plan. Veterans were left destitute, and Hamilton did benefit financially. But few policy decisions are without negative consequences, and these facts without more aren't enough to eliminate Hamilton as a threat. Jefferson needs external evidence to ruin Hamilton's reputation.
- Jefferson is perceived as Hamilton's leading political antagonist in the second half of the story, particularly in this

scene. However, it's important to remember the difference between a story's main (global) antagonist and the scene-to-scene bad guys. While Jefferson is undoubtedly a major problem here, Burr is the ultimate villain.

- Don't overlook how active and confident Burr is becoming in the story. Now that he's taken some action and is a Senator from New York, his envy and bitterness about Hamilton's success is increasingly manifested externally. Burr wants to be a part of Hamilton's demise and adopts Jefferson and Madison's perspective that Hamilton doesn't deserve his success when he's behaved so poorly. Why else would Burr resort to name calling? He is desperate to understand why Hamilton thrives when he doesn't, and he can begin to understand only by joining Hamilton's enemies' investigation of Hamilton's behaviors.

- **A note on Irreconcilable Goods Crises:** A lot of writers who fully understand a best bad choice struggle to understand an irreconcilable goods choice. It's a common challenge. And honestly, sometimes it's a very close call. This scene is a great example to help clarify the difference between a best bad choice and irreconcilable goods choice. Essentially, an irreconcilable goods choice is the inverse of a best bad choice. The outcome will create negative consequences for others but not necessarily the character making the decision. There are some risks for Jefferson, Madison, and Burr in investigating the money in the Treasury, but very little. The outcome of their decision creates far more peril for Hamilton. See how this works?

"ONE LAST TIME"

SCENE 28

SUMMARY

In a meeting with Washington, Hamilton learns that Jefferson resigned to run for president. Hamilton sees this as an opportunity to strike out at Jefferson, but Washington has decided to resign. He asks that Hamilton draft a final speech to pass along the knowledge he's gained.

Hamilton is confused and protests that the time is not right, but Washington is concerned with the future and ensuring the fragile new nation survives them. Hamilton finally agrees, and with his help, Washington delivers his farewell address with an accounting of accomplishments, mistakes, and suggestions for the future.

ANALYZING THE SCENE

STORY EVENT

A Story Event is an active change of a universal human value for one or more characters as a result of conflict (one character's desires clash with another's, or an environmental shift changes the value positively or negatively).

A Working Scene contains at least one Story Event. To determine a scene's Story Event, answer these four Socratic questions:

1. What are the characters literally doing—that is, what are their micro on-the-surface actions?

Washington and Hamilton discuss Washington's decision to step down from the presidency.

2. What is the essential tactic of the characters—that is, what above-the-surface macro behaviors are they employing that are linked to a universal human value?

Washington wants to retire and live out his final years in peace while also teaching the nation how to move on so that the government does not die with one leader. Hamilton wants Washington to continue to serve as president. This leads to their rationalization of mistakes, his successes, and the good that will come from Washington's departure, thus, providing the nation with an example of a peaceful transfer of power.

3. What beyond-the-surface universal human values have changed for one or more characters in the scene? Which one of those value changes is most important and should be included in the Story Grid Spreadsheet?

Hamilton argues with Washington about his choice to resign as president. He tries to convince Washington to stay on but finally understands and respects Washington's perspective. Hamilton drafts Washington's farewell address. Washington's absence will leave Hamilton vulnerable.

Protected to Vulnerable

4. The Scene Event Synthesis: What Story Event sums up the scene's on-the-surface actions, essential above-the-surface worldview behavioral tactics, and beyond-the-surface value change? We will enter that event in the Story Grid Spreadsheet.

Washington explains his reasons for resigning, which Hamilton finally accepts.

HOW THE SCENE ABIDES BY THE FIVE COMMANDMENTS OF STORYTELLING

Inciting Incident: Causal. Washington warns Hamilton that Jefferson resigned.

Turning Point Progressive Complication: Revelatory. Washington explains to Hamilton that by stepping down, the nation learns to move on after he dies.

Crisis: Best bad choice. Hamilton can reject Washington's request to draft his farewell address, or he can support his mentor's decision.

Climax: Hamilton respects and admires Washington's decision and drafts Washington's farewell address, which Washington shares with the people.

Resolution: Washington retires to Mount Vernon, leaving Hamilton vulnerable and Jefferson and other candidates a chance to seek the presidency.

NOTES

- Having Washington in power benefits Hamilton, especially since—as Jefferson suggested—Hamilton wouldn't be in his position if not for Washington's support. Once he leaves, the nation learns to move on, but Hamilton's status is threatened by whoever takes his place.

- Hamilton's reaction to Washington's news is common for a Status Tragic character, a striving protagonist who fails to heed the lessons their mentors try to teach them. Since the opening number informed us that Hamilton dies, we can anticipate that he won't escape his flaws and sins.
- Surrendering power for a peaceful transfer is one of the great features of democracy, a governmental tradition that might not have existed without Washington's choice. This scene is a defining moment for Washington's character— and Hamilton's. Washington sacrifices power for the future of his country. Likewise, we get a glimpse of Hamilton's potential to mature and evolve. While resistant to Washington's choice at the beginning of the scene, Hamilton eventually drafts an address that shows he respects Washington's decision to step down. He reveals many similarities between Washington and himself. Both men hope for a free government, which inevitably makes them sympathetic despite their mistakes. If Hamilton remembers this going forward, there's hope he can grow as a leader and as an individual. Hamilton's respect of Washington's action gives us a glimpse of the leader Hamilton could become if he could follow Washington's example of self-esteem and putting others before his own status and power.

"I KNOW HIM" AND "THE ADAMS ADMINISTRATION"

SCENE 29

SUMMARY

"I Know Him" and "The Adams Administration" combine to form one scene.

King George III is shocked that Washington is resigning. The king wonders who will become president and quickly learns that John Adams has been elected. The monarch is delighted, confident that the country will destroy Adams and itself.

Once Adams takes charge, Jefferson, as his vice president, fires Hamilton. In private, Adams insults Hamilton, who responds with a public statement to humiliate Adams.

Madison celebrates because Hamilton has no position in the government and his reckless behavior destroyed Adams, the only viable candidate of the opposition.

But Jefferson is concerned Hamilton could still be a threat and says it's time to reveal the results of their investigation.

ANALYZING THE SCENE

STORY EVENT

A Story Event is an active change of a universal human value for one or more characters as a result of conflict (one character's desires clash with another's, or an environmental shift changes the value positively or negatively).

A Working Scene contains at least one Story Event. To determine a scene's Story Event, answer these four Socratic questions:

1. What are the characters literally doing—that is, what are their micro on-the-surface actions?

King George III learns that Washington has stepped down and that Adams is replacing him as president. Adams fires Hamilton who responds while Jefferson, Madison, and Burr plot against him.

2. What is the essential tactic of the characters—that is, what above-the-surface macro behaviors are they employing that are linked to a universal human value?

Hamilton wants to humiliate Adams. Jefferson, Madison, and Burr want Hamilton eliminated. Hamilton's crude and public response to Adams gives them this opportunity.

3. What beyond-the-surface universal human values have changed for one or more characters in the scene? Which one of those value changes is most important and should be included in the Story Grid Spreadsheet?

Hamilton falls from power and status almost immediately after Washington steps down. Adams is elected president and fires Hamilton, who lashes out and insults Adams in the press, further damaging his career. Hamilton is out of control, and Jefferson, Madison, and Burr recognize this.

4. The Scene Event Synthesis: What Story Event sums up the scene's on-the-surface actions, essential above-the-surface worldview behavioral tactics, and beyond-the-surface value change? We will enter that event in the Story Grid Spreadsheet.

King George III ponders how Washington could step down. John Adams becomes president and fires Hamilton, who publishes his response.

HOW THE SCENE ABIDES BY THE FIVE COMMANDMENTS OF STORYTELLING

Inciting Incident: Causal. John Adams succeeds George Washington as president.

Turning Point Progressive Complication: Active. John Adams fires Hamilton and insults him in private.

Crisis: Best bad choice. Hamilton can ignore the private insult or publish his response with the intent of ruining John Adams, the only other significant member of his party.

Climax: Hamilton publishes his response to John Adams and insinuates Adams is unequipped for the job.

Resolution: While this destroys Adams, a significant member of Hamilton's party, it also shows that Hamilton is out of control. Jefferson still sees Hamilton as a threat and convinces Madison and Burr that it's time to tell Hamilton what they know about Reynolds.

NOTES

- This is the active beginning of Hamilton's public fall from grace. Although still intelligent and articulate, he loses his temper after Adams fires and insults him. This threatens his credibility with his party, the Federalists, even though he probably experienced a momentary release by insulting Adams in the press. Hamilton's rash reaction to insult and his obsession with making this public sets up to an even worse public revelation soon. If Hamilton doesn't evolve as a character, if he refuses to forego his ego and gain self-esteem, he won't transform. And stories with characters who don't transform inevitably end as a cautionary tale.

- Although Adams looms large in this period of American history, his role in this story is limited to his impact on Hamilton's professional life. Writers must stay focused on the central dramatic questions and threads or they risk losing the real story and the audience. This can be tricky with historical fiction because the audience comes with their own ideas about what happened. You can't control that (any more than Hamilton could). What you can do is get clear on the story you want to tell and make sure each character in every scene supports that.

- Hamilton's action in this scene tosses Jefferson, Madison, and Burr a Crisis of their own. Should they confront Hamilton or not? This thread is picked up in the scene that follows.

"WE KNOW"
SCENE 30

SUMMARY

Jefferson, Madison, and Burr confront Hamilton with what they *think* they know. They believe Hamilton embezzled Treasury money to pay Reynolds, and they urge him to confess.

Hamilton didn't steal money entrusted to him. But he admits to a three-year affair with Maria and to paying Reynolds with his own money to keep it a secret. Hamilton offers to show Jefferson, Madison, and Burr the evidence if they promise to keep quiet. They agree.

After confirming they won't tell anybody, Jefferson and Madison leave. Burr hangs back. Hamilton seeks assurance that they won't use the affair against him. Burr answers, noncommittally, "rumors only grow."

ANALYZING THE SCENE

STORY EVENT

A Story Event is an active change of a universal human value for one or more characters as a result of conflict (one character's desires clash with another's, or an environmental shift changes the value positively or negatively).

A Working Scene contains at least one Story Event. To determine a scene's Story Event, answer these four Socratic questions:

1. What are the characters literally doing—that is, what are their micro on-the-surface actions?

Jefferson, Madison, and Burr confront Hamilton with what they think they know: Hamilton committed treason.

2. What is the essential tactic of the characters—that is, what above-the-surface macro behaviors are they employing that are linked to a universal human value?

Jefferson, Madison, and Burr attempt to get revenge on Hamilton for all the advantages they feel he has over them. They want to weaken him by forcing him to confess to treason. Hamilton hasn't committed treason and wants to clear his name. Instead, he tells them about his affair.

3. What beyond-the-surface universal human values have changed for one or more characters in the scene? Which one of those value changes is most important and should be included in the Story Grid Spreadsheet?

Hamilton works in his study undisturbed until the three men enter. They jump right to their reason for visiting. Hamilton knows he is vulnerable, seeing that he might risk failure if they accuse him of misappropriating government funds. He'd rather leave them with the truth. Jefferson and Madison leave with the promise that they won't tell anyone about Hamilton's affair, but Burr acts less convincingly—leaving Hamilton paranoid about what Burr might do.

Undisturbed to Paranoid

4. **The Scene Event Synthesis:** What Story Event sums up the scene's on-the-surface actions, essential above-the-surface worldview behavioral tactics, and beyond-the-surface value change? We will enter that event in the Story Grid Spreadsheet.

Jefferson, Madison, and Burr confront Hamilton about what they think is embezzlement, but Hamilton tells them about his affair instead because he's paranoid they'll ruin his reputation if he doesn't.

HOW THE SCENE ABIDES BY THE FIVE COMMANDMENTS OF STORYTELLING

Inciting Incident: Causal. Jefferson, Madison, and Burr agree to corner Hamilton with what they know.

Turning Point Progressive Complication: Revelatory. The three men accuse Hamilton of embezzling government funds.

Crisis: Best bad choice. Hamilton can deny the accusation and hope nothing comes of it or share what really happened if they promise not to tell anyone and risk them not following through with their end of the agreement.

Climax: Hamilton reveals records that document his payments to Reynolds from his own bank account to keep his affair with Maria quiet.

Resolution: Jefferson and Madison promise not to say anything, but Burr offers an ambiguous response. This leaves Hamilton paranoid about what people might say if the truth comes out.

NOTES

- "We Know" is the first of a four-scene sequence where Hamilton destroys himself and those he loves by using his own words against himself. Hamilton admits to shameful actions but hasn't committed an offense against the government or people of the United States. While Hamilton hasn't committed treason, this is just the beginning of his actions sullying his reputation.

- The way Hamilton handles this situation speaks volumes about his character. Despite his success, he hasn't been able to transform the way he sees the world and himself. On an external scale, Hamilton has gained power and status and attained several victories with his professional career. He has a wife and family who love him, yet he has not developed self-esteem and maturity. He can't see that the way he solved problems when he was "young, scrappy, and hungry," will cause him to lose everything.

- In "We Know," Hamilton is motivated to maintain his status, thinking he can protect his "good name" if he proves he paid Reynolds with his personal funds to cover up his infidelity. He misses the point. Solely focused on what he wants, he doesn't consider trying a different tactic—one that would better protect his family, particularly Eliza.

- In Hamilton's mind, there's never a time to adopt Burr's patience and ability to wait (though he employed Burr's "talk less and smile more" tactic in negotiations over the debt plan). Even though waiting and doing nothing would better serve his family and himself, he can't see it. This confrontation could have been an incident that no one ever brought up again, but he doesn't seem to consider that possibility.

- Although this scene kicks off the action and consequences that follow over the next three scenes, notice how each song in this sequence (starting with "We Know" and ending with "Burn") work as individual scenes not one giant scene. Why is this? Each scene contains a clear Turning Point Progressive Complication, Crisis, and Climax that cause a change in value for Hamilton, not just a change in behavior or tactics.

- When writing your own scenes, don't underestimate the

value of showing your readers how your protagonist acts on their Crisis. This is the moment readers or viewers want to see! We need to experience the Climax and Resolution (response to the Climax) of a scene in order to feel satisfied (pun intended), not just hear about it or feel rushed through such essential moments.

"HURRICANE"

SCENE 31

SUMMARY

Hamilton considers what he should do next given that Jefferson, Madison, and Burr could use his affair against him. He reminisces about the hurricane that destroyed his town and also provided the opportunity to write his way toward success. As a boy, his published description of the hurricane caught the attention of people who paid for his trip to America and college tuition. Hamilton also reflects on his mother's death from an illness that failed to kill Hamilton.

Burr's words, "Wait for it," echo in the darkness, but Hamilton ignores this warning and vows to write his way out of his predicament. Writing has saved him many times before. Subconscious warnings from Washington, Eliza, Angelica, and Maria remind Hamilton, "History has its eyes on you."

Hamilton ignores the potential consequences of writing about his affair. He assumes it's worse to wait and believes that his honesty will win people over and protect his legacy. He hurries to write the *Reynolds Pamphlet*.

ANALYZING THE SCENE

STORY EVENT

A Story Event is an active change of a universal human value for one or more characters as a result of conflict (one character's desires clash with another's, or an environmental shift changes the value positively or negatively).

A Working Scene contains at least one Story Event. To determine a scene's Story Event, answer these four Socratic questions:

1. What are the characters literally doing—that is, what are their micro on-the-surface actions?

Hamilton considers how to get himself out of his predicament while reminiscing about the past.

2. What is the essential tactic of the characters—that is, what above-the-surface macro behaviors are they employing that are linked to a universal human value?

Hamilton wants to protect his legacy and needs to figure out how best to do this.

3. What beyond-the-surface universal human values have changed for one or more characters in the scene? Which one of those value changes is most important and should be included in the Story Grid Spreadsheet?

Hamilton reflects on his life and concludes that writing has been both his salvation and reason for success. He assumes writing and publishing the *Reynolds Pamphlet* will protect his legacy. Many distant voices warn Hamilton to reconsider this plan, but he dismisses them, disillusioned and ignoring any potential consequences that could result from his actions. In Hamilton's mind, his problems are resolved.

Paranoid to Delusional

4. The Scene Event Synthesis: What Story Event sums up the scene's on-the-surface actions, essential above-the-surface worldview behavioral tactics, and beyond-the-surface value change? We will enter that event in the Story Grid Spreadsheet.

While reminiscing about his past and how far he's come in life—professionally and personally—Hamilton decides to confess his affair publicly.

HOW THE SCENE ABIDES BY THE FIVE COMMANDMENTS OF STORYTELLING

Inciting Incident: Causal. Burr reminds Hamilton that rumors only grow.

Turning Point Progressive Complication: Revelatory. Hamilton recalls that since his earliest days, writing has always improved his circumstances.

Crisis: Best bad choice. Hamilton can remain quiet and hope that Burr (or Jefferson and Madison) won't reveal his affair, or he can take his fate into his own hands by confessing to his mistakes, believing his honesty will protect his legacy.

Climax: Hamilton decides to write the *Reynolds Pamphlet* despite subconscious warnings from Washington, Eliza, Angelica, and Maria.

Resolution: Hamilton overlooks how this will create a difficult (if not tragic) marital situation.

NOTES

- Miranda notes that several motifs from earlier songs return as internal voices begging Hamilton to reconsider how his actions will impact and impair him and others.[1] Can you see how powerful it is to set up these moments earlier in the story and see them pay off in this way. This effect is another way to create surprising but inevitable endings. Here, these reminders evoke empathy in the audience because we know what it's like to be blind to our own acts of self-sabotage. Finally this scene illuminates how the recurring themes/phrases are threads we use to tie different parts of the story together into a cohesive whole.

- Notice how this scene centers around internal reflection, but since it's a musical we also get the visual representation of Hamilton's conversation with himself. What's even more interesting is the extreme challenge and complexity of this scene. Hamilton is alone and thinks about his whole life. We can see his revelation from "Alexander Hamilton" (scene 1) that he had to look out for himself because he was all alone echoes here. He fails to realize he's not alone now and that he has earned his success but not without the support and love of others including Eliza, Angelica, and Washington, but also Laurens, Lafayette, and Mulligan. They are all with him though they aren't physically present now. He lacks the perspective he could have gained by reaching out or even considering, what would Angelica or Washington do in this situation? At the center of Hamilton's fatal mistake is his failure to see and act on this truth.

---

1. McCarter and Miranda, *Hamilton: The Revolution*, 233n4.

"THE REYNOLDS PAMPHLET"

SCENE 32

SUMMARY

In a frenzy, Hamilton writes the *Reynolds Pamphlet*. Its publication ruins Hamilton's professional reputation and personal relationships.

After reading the *Reynolds Pamphlet*, most people are shocked, but Jefferson, Madison, and Burr rejoice at Hamilton's arrogance realizing this action will end his political career.

Angelica arrives from London, and Hamilton thinks she will understand him and back him up. She makes it clear she has returned to support Eliza.

Hamilton's defense that he was "honest with our money" is drowned out by others who mock him and bystanders who pity "his poor wife."

ANALYZING THE SCENE

STORY EVENT

A Story Event is an active change of a universal human value for one or more characters as a result of conflict (one character's desires clash with another's, or an environmental shift changes the value positively or negatively).

A Working Scene contains at least one Story Event. To determine a scene's Story Event, answer these four Socratic questions:

1. What are the characters literally doing—that is, what are their micro on-the-surface actions?

Hamilton publishes the *Reynolds Pamphlet,* and the people react to it.

2. What is the essential tactic of the characters—that is, what above-the-surface macro behaviors are they employing that are linked to a universal human value?

Hamilton wants to clear his name and protect his legacy. He remains blind to what publishing his confession will really do—create relentless gossip and public shaming. The people's horror at the pamphlet's contents, including Angelica and her decision to comfort Eliza and abandon Hamilton, demonstrate these extreme consequences.

3. What beyond-the-surface universal human values have changed for one or more characters in the scene? Which one of those value changes is most important and should be included in the Story Grid Spreadsheet?

Hamilton publishes the pamphlet confident that people will pardon him because of their respect for his honesty, but he is proven wrong. The American citizens are horrified at their nation's first sex scandal. They shame Hamilton with gossip. Hamilton fights back but nobody cares, not even Angelica. He has ruined his status and personal relationships as well as broken Eliza's heart.

Confident to Public and Personal Failure

4. The Scene Event Synthesis: What Story Event sums up the scene's on-the-surface actions, essential above-the-surface worldview behavioral tactics, and beyond-the-surface value change? We will enter that event in the Story Grid Spreadsheet.

People publicly shun Hamilton for his publication of the Reynolds Pamphlet.

HOW THE SCENE ABIDES BY THE FIVE COMMANDMENTS OF STORYTELLING

Inciting Incident: Causal. Hamilton publishes the *Reynolds Pamphlet.*

Turning Point Progressive Complication: Revelatory. Hamilton expresses gratitude for Angelica's arrival, but she rejects and abandons him.

Crisis: Best bad choice. Hamilton can try to convince Angelica that he published the *Reynolds Pamphlet* to regain his wife's trust and affection, or he can let her go.

Climax: Hamilton lets Angelica go and admits to public and personal shame.

Resolution: Hamilton loses the support from the people who most believed in him and is publicly shamed. Hamilton's professional and personal relationships are severely jeopardized, if not destroyed. The women who love him most, Eliza and Angelica, are brokenhearted.

NOTES

- In one fleeting day, everything Hamilton has earned comes crashing down. Hamilton's defense that at least he was "honest with our money" is drowned out by others who insult and mock him. His honesty may have cleared his conscience, but it also potentially corrupts his legacy. On top

147

of this, Hamilton breaks Eliza's heart, the person who respected, supported, and loved him most. As bystanders pity "his poor wife," Eliza prepares to do what will leave historians unsatisfyingly curious.

- Hamilton sabotages his reputation through writing (ironically, his greatest strength). However, the consequences for Hamilton's actions don't end with him. Some of the worst ramifications hurt those who loved and supported (and one who exploited) Hamilton the most: Eliza, Angelica, Washington, and Reynolds. Hamilton's arrogance finally results in several figurative deaths—just as Burr warned would happen back in their first encounter, with "Aaron Burr, Sir" and "My Shot" (setups paying off). Because of his failure to embrace esteem and admit to his wrongs in a healthy way, he falls. Fast and far.
- Look at how Jefferson, Madison, and Burr chant that Hamilton is "never gon' be president now." They keep their agreement, and still Hamilton goes down. He allows his paranoia and desperate need for third-party validation to convince him to write his own death sentence. All his antagonists can simply sit back and watch. This reinforces the cautionary lesson that a character who refuses to change and grow seals his own doom.
- Although technically Hamilton couldn't be elected president anyway (he was born outside the American colonies), the chanted lines give an extra swift punch to Hamilton's ego. There's little chance of Hamilton coming back from this, and it seems that Jefferson's worries about Hamilton and the power of his pen is eliminated. Hamilton's greatest strength destroys his reputation, so how might Hamilton employ this tool in the future? And what will the result be?

"BURN"

SCENE 33

SUMMARY

Having no suspicion of Hamilton's affair before the *Reynolds Pamphlet*, Eliza is humiliated and heartbroken following its release. She carries her letters, a bucket, and a candle into a dark room.

Eliza reflects on their courtship and the love they shared but also remembers Angelica's early warning that Hamilton would "do what it takes to survive."

By burning his letters that could have mitigated the damage, she ensures Hamilton's legacy won't be saved and extracts herself from his story. With her closing line, Eliza admits she hopes Hamilton, like her letters, will burn.

ANALYZING THE SCENE

STORY EVENT

A Story Event is an active change of a universal human value for one or more characters as a result of conflict (one character's desires clash with another's, or an environmental shift changes the value positively or negatively).

A Working Scene contains at least one Story Event. To determine a scene's Story Event, answer these four Socratic questions:

1. What are the characters literally doing—that is, what are their micro on-the-surface actions?

Eliza burns Hamilton's letters while reflecting on the past and thinking about the future.

2. What is the essential tactic of the characters—that is, what above-the-surface macro behaviors are they employing that are linked to a universal human value?

Hamilton wants to protect his reputation and legacy and ignores how his public confession hurts his wife and family. After Alexander's cruel publication, Eliza enters a dark room alone. She declares her intent to remove herself from the narrative and burns Hamilton's love letters.

3. What beyond-the-surface universal human values have changed for one or more characters in the scene? Which one of those value changes is most important and should be included in the Story Grid Spreadsheet?

Hamilton's and Eliza's reputations are ruined, and she is heartbroken. Alone, she reminisces about their past and future before calling him out for his paranoia. Enraged, embarrassed, and betrayed, Eliza decides to remove herself from Hamilton's and history's narrative. She burns his love letters.

Heartbroken to Enraged

4. The Scene Event Synthesis: What Story Event sums up the scene's

on-the-surface actions, essential above-the-surface worldview behavioral tactics, and beyond-the-surface value change? We will enter that event in the Story Grid Spreadsheet.

Eliza burns Hamilton's love letters to remove herself from history's narrative of him and his legacy.

HOW THE SCENE ABIDES BY THE FIVE COMMANDMENTS OF STORYTELLING

Inciting Incident: Causal. Hamilton publishes the *Reynolds Pamphlet*.

Turning Point Progressive Complication: Revelatory. Eliza realizes how paranoid and obsessed Hamilton was with his legacy.

Crisis: Best bad choice. Eliza can continue to love Hamilton and live as if nothing happened but forever feel distant and betrayed, or she can salvage the one thing she has control over, the knowledge of how she reacted to his public confession.

Climax: Eliza burns Hamilton's letters, permanently removing herself from history's narrative. She accepts they will no longer have the same relationship and vows that he has forfeited the rights to her heart and their bed.

Resolution: History will never know how Eliza reacted to the scandal. Eliza and Hamilton grow apart.

NOTES

- While this scene belongs to Eliza, it illustrates how fatal mistakes can cause disastrous repercussions and consequences for the protagonist and others, especially those they care about most. Much like in life.
- "Burn" is the final scene in the sequence that plays out how Hamilton sabotaged his status and reputation. Not only does

Hamilton lose his public professional success, but he also loses the love of his life. One of the most tragic elements of Hamilton's fall is that Eliza tried to show him that letting her into his life fully would offer a satisfying life. Unfortunately, his circumstances will get worse.

- "Burn" is one of the most haunting and empowering scenes in the story. Eliza is the kindest and most compassionate character in the story, and we really feel it when her heart is broken. It's important to realize moments like this don't just happen. They are crafted by establishing multidimensional characters through their desires, actions, and how other characters respond to them.

- Scene by scene from the beginning we form a picture of who Eliza is. We know she wants a deep emotional connection with her husband and children (and this evokes empathy in the audience). We understand the sacrifices she's willing to make for her loved ones. Angelica tells us Eliza would have given Hamilton up if her sister had asked. She doesn't care about Hamilton's wealth or position in society, but also doesn't shame Hamilton for wanting to pursue professional success. She's a devoted mother who cares about her son's relationship with his father. Knowing who she is, the tension builds from the time when Hamilton engages in the affair to when it becomes public. How will she react?

- While Angelica may be the first to come to mind when fans think about powerful female characters, Eliza is arguably the true hero of this story. She emanates an inner strength no other character rivals.

- When betrayed in public, Eliza acts in private, burning the love letters Hamilton sent her during their courtship. This quiet act is empowering because she seizes her agency. She decides whether the world gets to know her story. Legacy doesn't matter to Eliza, whereas it means *everything* to Hamilton. When she rejoins Hamilton's narrative at the end, we can see what a sacrifice she's making.

"BLOW US ALL AWAY"
SCENE 34

SUMMARY

Hamilton's shadow looms large over his son Philip when he graduates from King's College at nineteen. He possesses many of the same qualities that made his father successful. After George Eacker, a New York lawyer, badmouths Hamilton in a public speech, Philip seeks justice, demanding that Eacker apologize for the insult. When he refuses, Philip challenges him to a duel.

Philip turns to his father for advice. Hamilton walks Philip through the process and recommends that his son fire his weapon in the air. Eacker will do the same, he insists, and Eliza can't take another heartbreak.

At the duel, Philip raises his gun to the sky, like his father instructed him to do, but Eacker fires early. The bullet enters Philip's hip, and lodges in his right arm.

ANALYZING THE SCENE

STORY EVENT

A Story Event is an active change of a universal human value for one or more characters as a result of conflict (one character's desires clash with another's, or an environmental shift changes the value positively or negatively).

A Working Scene contains at least one Story Event. To determine a scene's Story Event, answer these four Socratic questions:

1. What are the characters literally doing—that is, what are their micro on-the-surface actions?

Philip challenges George Eacker to a duel. Hamilton offers advice.

2. What is the essential tactic of the characters—that is, what above-the-surface macro behaviors are they employing that are linked to a universal human value?

Philip wants to defend his father's legacy. Eacker wants to shut Philip up. Hamilton wants to mentor his son but also not lose him or hurt Eliza more than he already has.

3. What beyond-the-surface universal human values have changed for one or more characters in the scene? Which one of those value changes is most important and should be included in the Story Grid Spreadsheet?

Philip graduates from King's College with high honors and unlimited potential, but when Eacker insults Hamilton, Philip challenges him to a duel. Hamilton coaches Philip on what to do, including advising him to fire in the air. Eacker shoots Philip before the count of ten. Philip falls, severely injured.
Full of Potential to Imminent Death

4. The Scene Event Synthesis: What Story Event sums up the scene's on-the-surface actions, essential above-the-surface worldview

behavioral tactics, and beyond-the-surface value change? We will enter that event in the Story Grid Spreadsheet.

Hamilton's son, Philip, is shot when he defends his father's honor in a duel with Eacker.

HOW THE SCENE ABIDES BY THE FIVE COMMANDMENTS OF STORYTELLING

Inciting Incident: Causal. Eacker disparages Alexander Hamilton while speaking on the Fourth of July.

Turning Point Progressive Complication: Active. Philip challenges Eacker to a duel.

Crisis: Best bad choice. Philip can forsake the duel or take Hamilton's advice and participate in the duel but fire in the air.

Climax: Philip participates in the duel. Before they reach the count of ten, Philip aims his gun toward the sky.

Resolution: Eacker shoots him anyway, on the count of seven. Philip is shot and goes down.

NOTES

- Notice how Philip has no desire to shoot Eacker or participate in a duel, but Philip cares about his father's approval, and Hamilton cares about his legacy. Even so, neither expects Philip to die. The "Ten Duel Commandments," tells us that most disputes are resolved one way or another without death (setup). Hamilton relies on this this probability when advising his son. Unfortunately, both father and son consider legacy and honor over the risk of physical death, which contributes to their tragic demise (unexpected payoff).

- Hamilton mentions that Eliza can't take "another heartbreak" so Philip may not take Eacker's life. This truth is as cruel as it is tragic. Of course, Hamilton was responsible for that heartbreak.
- How would Eliza have responded? If Philip survives but shoots Eacker, she would have been upset. She's not one for egotistical stand-offs or the senseless waste of a life. So, Hamilton and Philip think the only way out of this is to either not attend the duel (which doesn't seem like an option for "honorable" men during this time), or deliberately miss. If your stomach doesn't turn at the potential tragic consequences of Philip's conundrum, it sure does when he salutes his nine-year-old self. Hamilton and Philip are blind to the risk to Philip's life.
- Philip's salute to his nine-year-old self (setup) draws our attention back to his innocence, but also that Philip wants to make his mark in the world. He's off to a great start as a graduate of King's College at nineteen. But his desire to please his father is motivating him here. While Philip believes he is defending Hamilton's honor by dueling (similar to Hamilton's participation in the Laurens-Lee duel), he doesn't consider that by risking death he might not live long enough to fulfill his potential (which really could blow us all away).

"STAY ALIVE (REPRISE)" AND "IT'S QUIET UPTOWN"

SCENE 35

SUMMARY

"Stay Alive (Reprise)" opens as Hamilton charges into the doctor's house to find Philp's wound is already infected as he lies in agony on a table. Hamilton tries to calm his son who struggles to explain that he did exactly as his father advised. Eliza enters, and the parents cradle their son until he dies.

In "It's Quiet Uptown," Hamilton moves his family uptown where he seeks relief and to uphold his family responsibilities. His grief lingers.

When Eliza appears on stage, Hamilton explains if they grieve together, they will be able to get through this loss. He asks if he could stay by her side, and confesses that if she lets him do this, that "would be enough," echoing her words when she first told him she was pregnant.

In the end, Eliza and Hamilton stand in the garden side by side, and she forgives her husband.

ANALYZING THE SCENE

STORY EVENT

A Story Event is an active change of a universal human value for one or more characters as a result of conflict (one character's desires clash with another's, or an environmental shift changes the value positively or negatively).

A Working Scene contains at least one Story Event. To determine a scene's Story Event, answer these four Socratic questions:

1. What are the characters literally doing—that is, what are their micro on-the-surface actions?

Alexander and Eliza, along with their surviving children, move uptown after Philip's death. They search for ways to bear their grief.

2. What is the essential tactic of the characters—that is, what above-the-surface macro behaviors are they employing that are linked to a universal human value?

Hamilton and Eliza want their son alive, but since they can't have this, they long to relieve their pain and find a way to move on. They hold on to their love and memories of Philip. To a certain extent, they are reconciling in their grief.

3. What beyond-the-surface universal human values have changed for one or more characters in the scene? Which one of those value changes is most important and should be included in the Story Grid Spreadsheet?

Hamilton's oldest son has died, leaving this world forever. Stuck in despair and desperate to find any path to healing, Hamilton moves his family uptown. He spends his days grieving and hopes Eliza can find a way to forgive him. Eventually, though grief stricken, she does. Hamilton moves further away from public success, but some hope of healing his marriage remains, thanks to Eliza's compassion and tenderness.

Failure to Forgiveness

4. The Scene Event Synthesis: What Story Event sums up the scene's on-the-surface actions, essential above-the-surface worldview behavioral tactics, and beyond-the-surface value change? We will enter that event in the Story Grid Spreadsheet.

After Philip dies, Hamilton moves his family uptown. Hamilton seeks and is given Eliza's forgiveness.

HOW THE SCENE ABIDES BY THE FIVE COMMANDMENTS OF STORYTELLING

Inciting Incident: Causal. Philip dies.

Turning Point Progressive Complication: Revelatory. Hamilton realizes Philip would have liked it uptown (he mentions Philip by name).

Crisis: Best bad choice. Hamilton can work through his unimaginable grief alone or try to gain Eliza's forgiveness and work through it together.

Climax: Hamilton asks for forgiveness from Eliza, and Eliza eventually takes his hand.

Resolution: Eliza forgives Alexander for his mistakes. They move forward as a reestablished (although still mourning) team.

NOTES

- Between "Blow Us All Away" and "It's Quiet Uptown" comes the reprise of "Stay Alive." In this song, Hamilton and Eliza rush to Philip's side and hold their son as he dies. In many scenes where there is a death, this often establishes the

Turning Point that creates a value shift (from Life to Death). But Philip's death does not force a clear Crisis. Philip's death is a further Resolution of Philip's decision to follow his father's advice ("Blow Us All Away") and Inciting Incident in the scene that concludes with "It's Quiet Uptown." Both scenes are tethered to Philip's death, which not only escalates the stakes but deepens Hamilton's and Eliza's pain. This is also why, on the spreadsheet, "Stay Alive (Reprise)" is combined with "It's Quiet Uptown."

- Hamilton seeks comfort and quiet for his wife and family. They move uptown (payoff) when he refused to even vacation upstate for a summer in "Take a Break" (setup). Hamilton assumes responsibilities he's never done before, like taking the kids to church. He comes to rely on the quiet.
- Eventually he asks for forgiveness from Eliza, and she grants it. By taking Alexander's hand, Eliza acknowledges that they each have a better chance of getting through the loss together. She has been trying to convince him of this for a long time, that whatever challenges come along, they can face them together. It seems he finally understands.
- Hamilton is far from success, but his marriage is salvaged, and he's attending to his family duties. We feel more sympathy for him. He's trying to be better.
- Angelica is a key figure in the Love Story subplot, and it makes sense for us to see this scene through her eyes. She is close enough to the people and events to care but has enough distance to direct our attention to what's important.

"THE ELECTION OF 1800"

SCENE 36

SUMMARY

Hamilton is absent from the political stage as the 1800 election approaches in which Jefferson runs for president against Burr.

Jefferson and Madison discuss options for persuading the Federalists, who have control of the House of Representatives, to select Jefferson over Burr. Madison suggests convincing Hamilton to endorse him because of his prior influence with the Federalists. Jefferson admits Hamilton's support might be his only chance to win.

Burr actively campaigns against Jefferson when he bumps into Hamilton. Burr says he's willing to do anything to get what he wants, a lesson he learned from Hamilton.

A tie between Burr and Jefferson means the Federalists will decide who will be the next president, and they turn to Hamilton for advice. Hamilton supports Jefferson, who becomes president and humiliates Burr by choosing someone else to be his vice president.

Burr grows angrier.

ANALYZING THE SCENE

STORY EVENT

A Story Event is an active change of a universal human value for one or more characters as a result of conflict (one character's desires clash with another's, or an environmental shift changes the value positively or negatively).

A Working Scene contains at least one Story Event. To determine a scene's Story Event, answer these four Socratic questions:

1. What are the characters literally doing—that is, what are their micro on-the-surface actions?

Burr and Jefferson run for president while Hamilton resides uptown.

2. What is the essential tactic of the characters—that is, what above-the-surface macro behaviors are they employing that are linked to a universal human value?

Burr and Jefferson compete for the presidency. Jefferson needs Hamilton's endorsement and works to earn it. Hamilton wants the future president to be someone who has a mind of his own. The people seek Hamilton's opinion on who should be president.

3. What beyond-the-surface universal human values have changed for one or more characters in the scene? Which one of those value changes is most important and should be included in the Story Grid Spreadsheet?

Initially a bystander in the scene, Hamilton resides uptown while Jefferson and Burr campaign for the presidency. Jefferson realizes he comes off as too extreme to the Federalists and seeks Hamilton's endorsement. Hamilton's endorsement influences the House of Representatives to elect Jefferson. Burr was hopeful but ends broken and feels betrayed.

Removed to Influential

4. The Scene Event Synthesis: What Story Event sums up the scene's on-the-surface actions, essential above-the-surface worldview behavioral tactics, and beyond-the-surface value change? We will enter that event in the Story Grid Spreadsheet.

Burr and Jefferson campaign for presidency while the Federalists look to Hamilton's endorsement before casting their electoral vote.

HOW THE SCENE ABIDES BY THE FIVE COMMANDMENTS OF STORYTELLING

Inciting Incident: Causal. Jefferson and Burr run for president.

Turning Point Progressive Complication: Active. The electoral vote results in a tie.

Crisis: Best bad choice. Hamilton can endorse Jefferson, a man he personally dislikes and disagrees with, or he can support Aaron Burr, a man Hamilton likes personally but also views as a weak governmental leader.

Climax: Hamilton endorses Jefferson, who is elected.

Resolution: Jefferson insults Burr and says he's changing the rules about who becomes vice president. Burr is left bitter and resentful and begins to blame Hamilton for his failures.

NOTES

- Hamilton's party members still respect his political and professional opinion on the presidential candidate. So Hamilton's status is slightly elevated here. This is another example of Hamilton being out of the spotlight. His focus on his family and what's important results in success.

- We can look at this scene from multiple points of view because we have characters whose desires are not compatible.

- In the beginning, things don't look good for Jefferson. He lacks support of the Federalists and will likely lose if he can't get Hamilton's endorsement for his candidacy. This forces him into a Crisis to ask for Hamilton's help or not. This plays out off stage.

- Meanwhile, Burr's chances look extremely favorable, and it's not until Hamilton endorses Jefferson that Burr's success takes a negative turn. This forces his own Crisis, which plays out in the next scene, "Your Obedient Servant."

- Despite Hamilton's being the least active character in the scene, his Climax has the greatest impact on everyone. A lot is going on in this scene, but the request for his input and Hamilton's decision to endorse Jefferson change the value in the scene.

- In most scenes, the Crisis is implied, and we don't see the character debating the pros and cons of each option. Readers and viewers don't need it spelled out because we're shown. Here, the best bad choice is stated clearly, and the voters know it. It works here in part because it's catchy, but the circumstances give them a strong reason to ask Hamilton and for him to decide.

"YOUR OBEDIENT SERVANT" AND "BEST OF WIVES AND BEST OF WOMEN"

SCENE 37

SUMMARY

Infuriated by Hamilton's endorsement of Jefferson, Burr writes a letter to blame his misfortunes on his rival and challenge him to speak directly.

Hamilton doesn't accept responsibility. Burr has employed his strategy so well that people don't know what he believes and therefore can't trust him. Endorsing Jefferson was the right thing to do, and Hamilton won't apologize because he speaks the truth.

Burr challenges Hamilton to a duel, and Hamilton agrees.

Eliza enters as Hamilton is writing the night before the duel. She asks him to come to bed. Hamilton insists he needs to finish his letter first. She accepts this. Before she leaves, Hamilton kisses her hand and tells her she is the "Best of wives and best of women."

ANALYZING THE SCENE

STORY EVENT

A Story Event is an active change of a universal human value for one or more characters as a result of conflict (one character's desires clash with another's, or an environmental shift changes the value positively or negatively).

A Working Scene contains at least one Story Event. To determine a scene's Story Event, answer these four Socratic questions:

1. What are the characters literally doing—that is, what are their micro on-the-surface actions?

Burr and Hamilton exchange letters demanding an apology (Burr) and refusing to do so (Hamilton).

2. What is the essential tactic of the characters—that is, what above-the-surface macro behaviors are they employing that are linked to a universal human value?

Burr wants Hamilton to apologize. Hamilton wants Burr to understand why he will not do so. He believes he is right to stand by his words. Because of this, Burr challenges Hamilton to a duel.

3. What beyond-the-surface universal human values have changed for one or more characters in the scene? Which one of those value changes is most important and should be included in the Story Grid Spreadsheet?

Burr breaks. Despite his place as vice president, he calls out Hamilton as the ultimate culprit for his professional failures and demands an apology. Hamilton refuses and instead accepts the duel. He writes his last letter late at night and experiences a particularly tender moment when he acknowledges Eliza as the "best of wives and best of women."

Success to Risk of Failure and Death

4. The Scene Event Synthesis: What Story Event sums up the scene's on-the-surface actions, essential above-the-surface worldview behavioral tactics, and beyond-the-surface value change? We will enter that event in the Story Grid Spreadsheet.

Burr and Hamilton exchange letters regarding Hamilton's disagreements and disrespect of Burr, and eventually Burr challenges Hamilton to a duel.

HOW THE SCENE ABIDES BY THE FIVE COMMANDMENTS OF STORYTELLING

Inciting Incident: Causal. Burr writes Hamilton a letter demanding an apology.

Turning Point Progressive Complication: Revelatory. Burr warns Hamilton that if he doesn't apologize, he will challenge him to a duel.

Crisis: Best bad choice. Hamilton can accept Burr's duel and defend his personal and political reputation or reject the duel.

Climax: Burr challenges Hamilton to a duel and Hamilton accepts. Burr and Hamilton prepare for the duel.

Resolution: Hamilton works late into the night, despite Eliza's request that he come back to bed. He declines but tells Eliza that she is the "Best of wives and best of women."

NOTES

- As an audience, we begin to realize Eliza will be the one to carry Hamilton's legacy after he's gone. We feel anticipatory catharsis because we know what this means.
- "Your Obedient Servant" is the last straw for Burr. In his accounting of their relationship, he realizes he can no longer take Hamilton's disrespect of his style of ambition. He acts boldly here, challenging Hamilton to a duel, which looking

from the outside is clearly not his best option. He couldn't have hoped to gain anything meaningful as a result. It represents the choice to put ambition and ego ahead of life. He can't see this or how he contributes to his own failure.

- Hamilton's choice to participate is not better. If Eliza couldn't bear more heartache before Philip's death, what would be her reaction now? And what would he suffer by simply letting it drop? Even after his disgrace, he was called upon to choose the next president. What could he have accomplished had he not thrown away his shot here?

- We know Burr is the villain in Hamilton's history, though Hamilton is responsible too. Burr demands the duel, and Hamilton accepts.

- Viewers can see themselves in both Burr and Hamilton. We've all been passed over by professional strivers in our own fields, and we've all experienced victories where we sacrificed much to achieve. Ignoring the duality blinds us to the potential tragedy if we cannot manage our pride and embrace self-respect, rather than living by society's definition of our success—a classic Status cautionary tale if there ever was one.

- We can analyze this scene from the perspective of Burr's Crisis too. Burr could drop his demand and accept Hamilton's obstinance or challenge him to a duel to settle their differences, which risks both their lives.

"THE WORLD WAS WIDE ENOUGH"

SCENE 38

SUMMARY

After the duel preliminaries, Burr and Hamilton face each other across a field near where Philip fought and lost his duel. Unable to reach an impasse, the seconds withdraw. Burr can't read Hamilton's intention in his actions but concludes he will not allow his daughter to become orphan. Burr fires.

Hamilton contemplates his life seeing the loved ones who died before him as well as Eliza. Then he aims his gun in the air. Too late to reverse what's been done, Burr realizes he should have waited.

Hamilton and Burr lose everything they've earned.

ANALYZING THE SCENE

STORY EVENT

A Story Event is an active change of a universal human value for one or more characters as a result of conflict (one character's desires clash with another's, or an environmental shift changes the value positively or negatively).

A Working Scene contains at least one Story Event. To determine a scene's Story Event, answer these four Socratic questions:

1. What are the characters literally doing—that is, what are their micro on-the-surface actions?

Burr and Hamilton prepare for and fight in a duel.

2. What is the essential tactic of the characters—that is, what above-the-surface macro behaviors are they employing that are linked to a universal human value?

Burr initially enters the duel for revenge, and Hamilton, despite not wanting to die, intends to throw away his shot, even though he refuses to negotiate.

3. What beyond-the-surface universal human values have changed for one or more characters in the scene? Which one of those value changes is most important and should be included in the Story Grid Spreadsheet?

Hamilton and Burr take their places in the duel. Burr becomes increasingly angry and more certain that Hamilton intends to shoot. Hamilton debates whether throwing away his shot is the right decision. Burr shoots Hamilton, and he dies. Burr is marked as the villain in Hamilton's history.

Refusal to Compromise to Failure

4. The Scene Event Synthesis: What Story Event sums up the scene's on-the-surface actions, essential above-the-surface worldview behavioral tactics, and beyond-the-surface value change? We will enter that event in the Story Grid Spreadsheet.

Hamilton contemplates his legacy right before deciding to delope. Burr shoots and kills him.

HOW THE SCENE ABIDES BY THE FIVE COMMANDMENTS OF STORYTELLING

Inciting Incident: Causal. Hamilton and Burr arrive at the site of the duel.

Turning Point Progressive Complication: Active. Hamilton and Burr refuse to negotiate.

Crisis: Best bad choice. Hamilton can throw away his shot and risk history remembering his legacy as nothing but this bullet, or he can shoot Burr and live with his action.

Climax: Hamilton fires into the air and away from Burr.

Resolution: Burr shoots Hamilton, killing him, and is told to hide. History could easily remember Hamilton by the shot he threw away. Meanwhile, Burr is considered the villain.

NOTES

- The obvious value shift in this scene is from life to death. But why aren't we putting this in the spreadsheet? Multiple shifts happen in any scene, but we focus on how the global value is enhanced. For a Status Story that is the Failure-Success gradient of value. Hamilton's death suggests that he fails completely, but we need to look again at what this means. Hamilton willingly throws away his shot and guarantees he will spare Burr's life. He risks his own life with no certainty that history will view him in a positive light. This is an act of sacrifice based on what they have meant to each other in the past.
- Why would he think this when he has so much more he

wants to accomplish? Hamilton lacks esteem and never gets what he needs. He can't let go of how history will view him and wishes he could control this. A hypothetical Hamilton with self-esteem says no to the duel because he wouldn't care about the story strangers tell about what he does. He would care about being of service to his family and nation and put this above all else. Hamilton remains unsatisfied but he doesn't end the story a villain, like Burr.

- Burr faces a Crisis here as well. He can shoot Hamilton and risk whatever consequences follow, like killing his friend and a respected politician, or he can allow Hamilton to get away with poisoning his political pursuits. He regrets shooting Hamilton immediately, but of course this insight is too late. Only after Hamilton is dead does Burr realize, "The world was wide enough for both him and me." We pity Burr, who lacked adequate mentors and felt robbed and cheated by Hamilton enough to challenge him to a duel. We don't forgive him for his decision to shoot, but we also understand his position up to this point. It's a sad reality that Burr spends the remainder of his life marked as a villain and Hamilton's killer.

- Hamilton does have adequate mentors such as Washington, Eliza, and Angelica. At times, he considers and listens to their advice. But ultimately, Hamilton forsakes warnings and advice for what he believes is best, even if it jeopardizes the well-being of others. Hamilton never fully grasps the concept that history has its eyes on him, and he can't control history's perception.

- This is a defining element of the Status Tragic subgenre. Our hero, having started low, rises up, and falls in the end. Eliza is left to defend and carry on his work.

- Meanwhile, Burr transforms as the waiting man who starts high and ends low, the friend turned villain of Alexander Hamilton's tragic arc.

- Subgenre Distinction: A protagonist who dies at the end of a Status Story doesn't necessarily mean we have a cautionary tale. The test is whether the protagonist achieves what they need (esteem) despite other people's opinion of them. A great example of this is *Gladiator*, the 2000 film directed by Ridley Scott and written by David Franzoni, John Logan, and William Nicholson. In this story, Maximus dies but he possesses esteem and honor, a requirement for a Status Admiration story.

- Hamilton's concern about his legacy and how history will remember him means he never fully possesses esteem. He can't accept Washington's words of wisdom that no one can control what other people think or say about themselves. Hamilton dies honorably by sparing his friend, but also because third-party validation is more important than his life and work.
- If we consider Hamilton's global value shift in the story, we remember how he moved from an ambitious and striving young man to a respected but unsatisfied founding leader of the country.

"WHO LIVES, WHO DIES, WHO TELLS YOUR STORY?"

SCENE 39

SUMMARY

Washington reminds the audience of the lesson he shared with Hamilton before the Battle of Yorktown. "You have no control: Who lives, who dies, who tells your story?"

While Hamilton's rivals attempt to bend his story to their own ends, Eliza emerges to set the record straight and fulfill the promise of his life by achieving things his death prevented, helping to construct the Washington Monument, campaigning against slavery, and opening an orphanage.

Eliza shares her longing for her husband, and Hamilton, in spirit, comes to her. He takes her hands and leads her to the edge of the stage. He and the company sing the question we wonder long after *Hamilton* ends. "Who lives, who dies, who tells your story?"

ANALYZING THE SCENE

STORY EVENT

A Story Event is an active change of a universal human value for one or more characters as a result of conflict (one character's desires clash with another's, or an environmental shift changes the value positively or negatively).

A Working Scene contains at least one Story Event. To determine a scene's Story Event, answer these four Socratic questions:

1. What are the characters literally doing—that is, what are their micro on-the-surface actions?

In response to Washington's question, Hamilton's enemies and loved ones tell his story. His enemies grudgingly admit his contributions, and Eliza saves Hamilton's legacy by defending his life achievements and fulfilling incomplete endeavors.

2. What is the essential tactic of the characters—that is, what above-the-surface macro behaviors are they employing that are linked to a universal human value?

Eliza wants Hamilton's legacy to be known by future generations. She also wants to accomplish dreams he didn't complete before his untimely death.

3. What beyond-the-surface universal human values have changed for one or more characters in the scene? Which one of those value changes is most important and should be included in the Story Grid Spreadsheet?

Eliza goes from bystander to defender of Hamilton's legacy. His enemies are free to discredit his accomplishments, but by telling his story and pursuing unfinished projects, Eliza ensures they don't have the last word. She defends Hamilton's legacy for the next fifty years of her life so that future generations still know of his deeds in founding the nation.

4. The Scene Event Synthesis: What Story Event sums up the scene's on-the-surface actions, essential above-the-surface worldview behavioral tactics, and beyond-the-surface value change? We will enter that event in the Story Grid Spreadsheet.

Eliza defends Hamilton's achievements, which his enemies try to erase, by sharing his story and fulfilling good acts he didn't live to complete.

HOW THE SCENE ABIDES BY THE FIVE COMMANDMENTS OF STORYTELLING

Inciting Incident: Causal. Hamilton's enemies (Jefferson and Madison) try to discredit Hamilton's successes.

Turning Point Progressive Complication: Revelatory. Eliza realizes that if she doesn't defend Hamilton's work, nobody will.

Crisis: Best bad choice. Eliza can allow grief to overtake her and accept that Hamilton's legacy will end with his life, or she can fight to protect it.

Climax: Eliza sets her grief aside to accomplish Hamilton's unfinished business and save the memory of his good works. Angelica helps her with this for as long as she lives, and when Angelica dies, she is buried in Trinity Church near Hamilton.

Resolution: Hamilton's legacy is saved thanks to her efforts. Eliza departs this world fifty years after his death. It's assumed she meets Hamilton in heaven.

NOTES

- To open this scene, Washington reminds the audience of the lesson he shared with Hamilton before the Battle of Yorktown. "You have no control: Who lives, who dies, who tells your story?" Hamilton's enemies outlived him and were fortunate enough to see how their contributions altered history. Hamilton does not have this opportunity, and many of his enemies sought to obscure his achievements. His story could have been left to these men who despised him.

- Eliza's efforts provide balance and ensure Hamilton's work is not lost to history. She continues to work on projects close to Hamilton's heart. She is, and forever remains, his constant. Eliza shares her longing for her husband, and Hamilton, in spirit, comes to her. He takes her hands and leads her to the edge of the stage. He and the company sing the question we wonder long after *Hamilton* ends. "Who lives, who dies, who tells your story?"

- Because Eliza defends Hamilton's life achievements and continues to pursue his dreams, she saves Hamilton's legacy. This unconventional ending works because Miranda brilliantly sets up Eliza's motivation to protect and honor Hamilton's good name. She never cares about status or how she'll be remembered. She's always possessed esteem, but she loves and appreciates Hamilton for who he is. She dedicates the remainder of her life by tethering her legacy (her narrative) permanently to her husband's out of pure, unconditional love.

- Hamilton's death is tragic, but it isn't meaningless. We're left with hope for Hamilton's success because his legacy and the lessons of his life will be more than a bullet he threw away. This creates a positive shift in the Status Story value toward Success, even though he doesn't survive.

- Great stories must entertain us first, but they go much further. They offer wisdom and advice to help us navigate life's uncertainties. Stories that go the extra mile also leave us with useful questions. In a story filled with prescriptive and cautionary examples for how to live life, the implied question we take with us from *Hamilton* is, given that you can't control the story that lives after you're gone, how will you spend the life you have?

ABOUT THE AUTHOR

Abigail K. Perry is a Certified Story Grid Editor with professional teaching, literary agency, and film production experience. As a stay-at-home mom, editor, writer, and advocate, Abigail is dedicated to helping students and writers develop a life-long passion for learning, reading, and creative writing. She does this with her day job as a developmental and diagnostic freelance editor and book coach, and as a writer of Story Grid Masterwork Guides and YA and adult fiction novels. Abigail deeply believes in empowering unique, diverse voices through storytelling and shares her 10+ years of experience in publishing, teaching, and production with her writing workshops (on Outlines, Women's Fiction, YA Fantasy, Upmarket Fiction, and Scripts), podcasts STORY EFFECT and SLUSH PILE SURVIVOR, and monthly columns for DIY MFA. To learn more about Abigail's editing services and writing, visit her website at www.abigailkperry.com.

ABOUT THE EDITOR

Sheila Lischwe, PhD, is a Certified Story Grid Editor based in South Carolina. She earned a doctoral degree in higher education administration from Saint Louis University and a master's degree in Writing, Rhetoric and Media at Clemson University. Dr. Lischwe has served as editor of *Research Management Review*, a professional peer-reviewed journal, and is working steadily on her first novel, a thriller, set in Upstate New York and a Story Grid Masterworks Analysis Guide of *Presumed Innocent* by Scott Turow. Her editing practice specializes in helping aspiring authors master Story Grid principles to create compelling works of fiction and nonfiction for publication.